GRADE K-1 45 Days of Kumon

finishing each day's math and reading exercises, paste a sticker in the appropriate place below. Make a note of any questions or difficulties in the blank space provided so you can review them later. You can also note what you learned or that day's accomplishment.

To parents: If your child seems to be having difficulty pasting the stickers or writing the date or notes, you can offer to help. When he or she has completed all of the pages, offer lots of praise and paste the biggest sticker under "Goal!" Finally, please fill out your child's name and sign your name along the bottom.

How to use this sheet

Keep your skills sharp all summer long!

Date / /

Math | Reading

1

- Paste a sticker here for completing a math exercise.
- Paste a sticker here for completing a reading exercise.
- Write about your questions, difficulties or accomplishments here.

Date / /	Date / /	Date / /	Date / /	Date / /	Date / /	Date / /
Math Reading	Math Reading	Math Reading	Math Reading	Math Reading	Math Reading	Math Reading
1	2	3	4	5	6	7

Date / /	Date / /	Date / /	Date / /	Date / /	Date / /	Date / /	Date / /	Date / /	Date / /
Math Reading	Math Reading	Math Reading	Math Reading	Math Reading	Math Reading	Math Reading	Math Reading	Math Reading	Math Reading
8	9	10	11	12	13	14	15	16	17

Date / /	Date / /	Date / /	Date / /	Date / /	Date / /	Date / /	Date / /	Date / /	Date / /
Math Reading	Math Reading	Math Reading	Math Reading	Math Reading	Math Reading	Math Reading	Math Reading	Math Reading	Math Reading
18	19	20	21	22	23	24	25	26	27

Date / /	Date / /	Date / /	Date / /	Date / /	Date / /	Date / /	Date / /	Date / /	Date / /
Math Reading	Math Reading	Math Reading	Math Reading	Math Reading	Math Reading	Math Reading	Math Reading	Math Reading	Math Reading
28	29	30	31	32	33	34	35	36	37

Date / /	Date / /	Date / /	Date / /	Date / /	Date / /	Date / /	Date / /
Math Reading	Math Reading	Math Reading	Math Reading	Math Reading	Math Reading	Math Reading	Math Reading
38	39	40	41	42	43	44	45

Goal!

_____ is hereby congratulated on completing Summer Review & Prep K-1. Presented on _____ , 20____

PARENT OR GUARDIAN _____

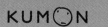

Kumon Summer Reading List

GRADE K-1

This list is designed to include a variety of genres, writing styles, cultures and authors.
Please use this list as a guide for reading during the summer.

How to use this list

- Write the date you start reading the book.
- Write the date you finish reading the book.
- Write your opinions and/or questions about the book.
- Aim to read all ten books during the summer.

TO PARENTS:
The Kumon Summer Reading List is designed to encourage children to develop independent reading skills. Children who acquire strong reading skills often enjoy a more successful and enriching educational experience. This list offers suggestions for quality books for readers between kindergarten and 1st grade. Please encourage your child to visit the library for more books.

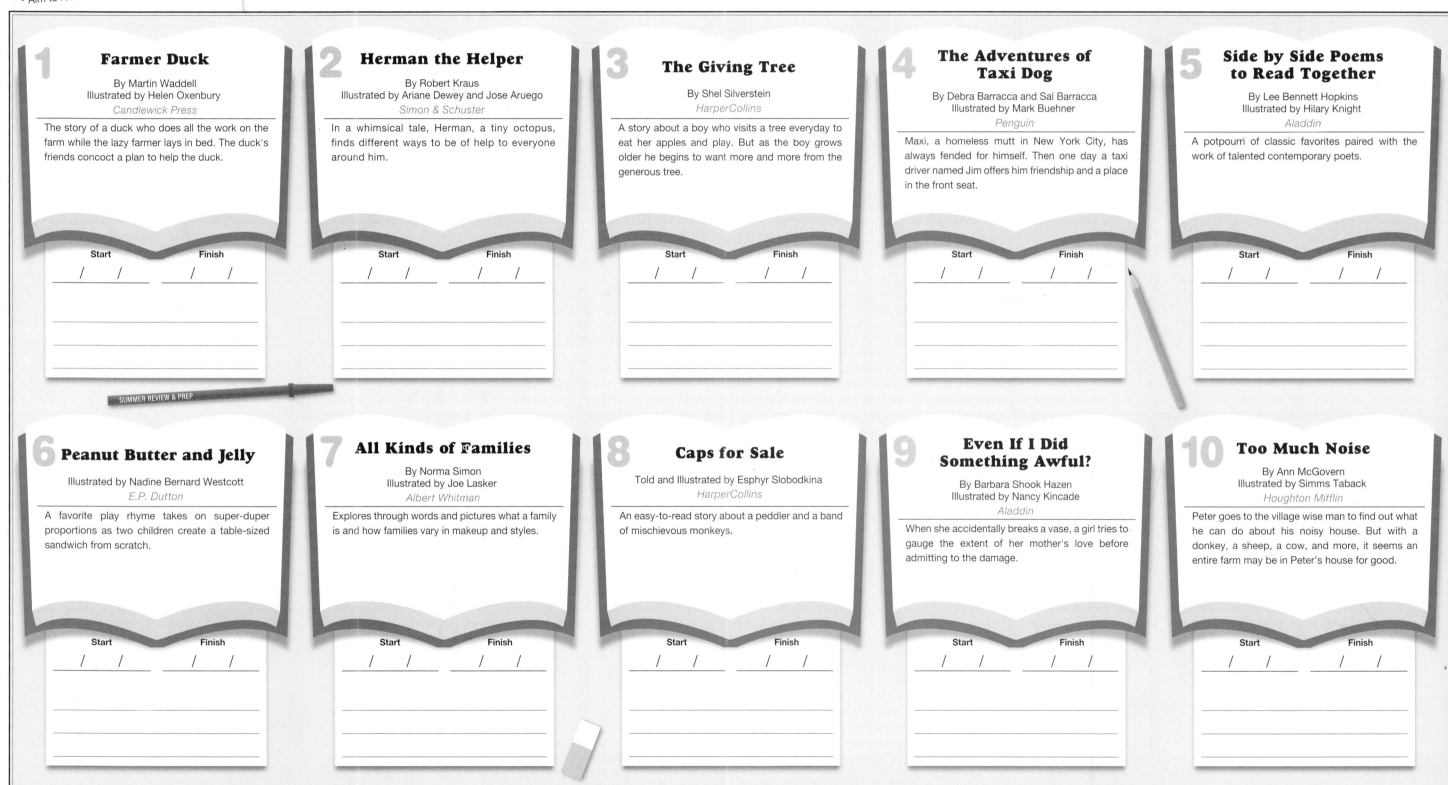

1 Farmer Duck
By Martin Waddell
Illustrated by Helen Oxenbury
Candlewick Press

The story of a duck who does all the work on the farm while the lazy farmer lays in bed. The duck's friends concoct a plan to help the duck.

Start / /   Finish / /

2 Herman the Helper
By Robert Kraus
Illustrated by Ariane Dewey and Jose Aruego
Simon & Schuster

In a whimsical tale, Herman, a tiny octopus, finds different ways to be of help to everyone around him.

Start / /   Finish / /

3 The Giving Tree
By Shel Silverstein
HarperCollins

A story about a boy who visits a tree everyday to eat her apples and play. But as the boy grows older he begins to want more and more from the generous tree.

Start / /   Finish / /

4 The Adventures of Taxi Dog
By Debra Barracca and Sal Barracca
Illustrated by Mark Buehner
Penguin

Maxi, a homeless mutt in New York City, has always fended for himself. Then one day a taxi driver named Jim offers him friendship and a place in the front seat.

Start / /   Finish / /

5 Side by Side Poems to Read Together
By Lee Bennett Hopkins
Illustrated by Hilary Knight
Aladdin

A potpourri of classic favorites paired with the work of talented contemporary poets.

Start / /   Finish / /

6 Peanut Butter and Jelly
Illustrated by Nadine Bernard Westcott
E.P. Dutton

A favorite play rhyme takes on super-duper proportions as two children create a table-sized sandwich from scratch.

Start / /   Finish / /

7 All Kinds of Families
By Norma Simon
Illustrated by Joe Lasker
Albert Whitman

Explores through words and pictures what a family is and how families vary in makeup and styles.

Start / /   Finish / /

8 Caps for Sale
Told and Illustrated by Esphyr Slobodkina
HarperCollins

An easy-to-read story about a peddler and a band of mischievous monkeys.

Start / /   Finish / /

9 Even If I Did Something Awful?
By Barbara Shook Hazen
Illustrated by Nancy Kincade
Aladdin

When she accidentally breaks a vase, a girl tries to gauge the extent of her mother's love before admitting to the damage.

Start / /   Finish / /

10 Too Much Noise
By Ann McGovern
Illustrated by Simms Taback
Houghton Mifflin

Peter goes to the village wise man to find out what he can do about his noisy house. But with a donkey, a sheep, a cow, and more, it seems an entire farm may be in Peter's house for good.

Start / /   Finish / /

SUMMER REVIEW & PREP

Counting Numbers 1 to 10

Level ★

Score

/100

1 Draw a line from 1 to 10 in order while saying each number aloud.

100 points for completion

| 1 | 2 | 3 | 4 | 5 | 6 | 7 | 8 | 9 | 10 |

(sailboat)

Reading
DAY
1

Uppercase Letters
"A" to "Z"

Level ★

Score

/100

Date
/   /

Name

---

① While saying each letter aloud, draw a line from A to Z to connect the letters in alphabetical order.

100 points for comple

| A | B | C | D | E | F | G | H | I | J | K | L | M | N | O | P | Q | R | S | T | U | V | W | X | Y | Z |

(fish)

© Kumon Publishing Co.,Ltd.

2

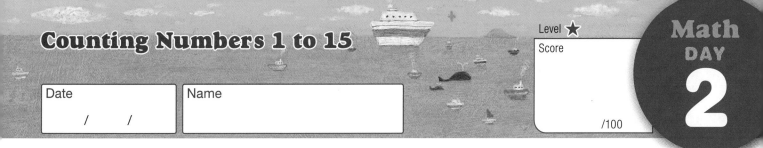

Counting Numbers 1 to 15

 Draw a line from 1 to 15 in order while saying each number aloud.

100 points for completion

| 1 | 2 | 3 | 4 | 5 | 6 | 7 | 8 | 9 | 10 | 11 | 12 | 13 | 14 | 15 |

(campfire)

Uppercase Letters
"A" to "Z"

Date   /   /

Name

(1) While saying each letter aloud, draw a line from A to Z to connect the letters in alphabetical order.

100 points for comple

| A | B | C | D | E | F | G | H | I | J | K | L | M | N | O | P | Q | R | S | T | U | V | W | X | Y | Z |

(whale)

Counting Numbers 1 to 20

Level ★

Score

Date / /

Name

/100

Math
DAY
3

1 Draw a line from 1 to 20 in order while saying each number aloud.

100 points for completion

| 1 | 2 | 3 | 4 | 5 | 6 | 7 | 8 | 9 | 10 | 11 | 12 | 13 | 14 | 15 | 16 | 17 | 18 | 19 | 20 |

(dolphin)

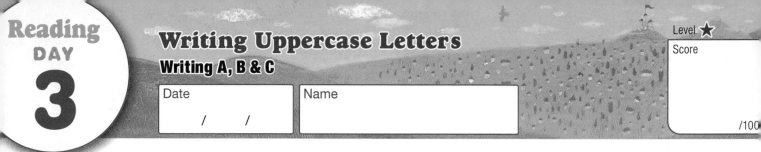

Writing Uppercase Letters
Writing A, B & C

Level ★
Score
/100

① Say the name of each letter. Then say the sound of the letter as you trace it. Follow the stroke order indicated by the numbers.

100 points for comple

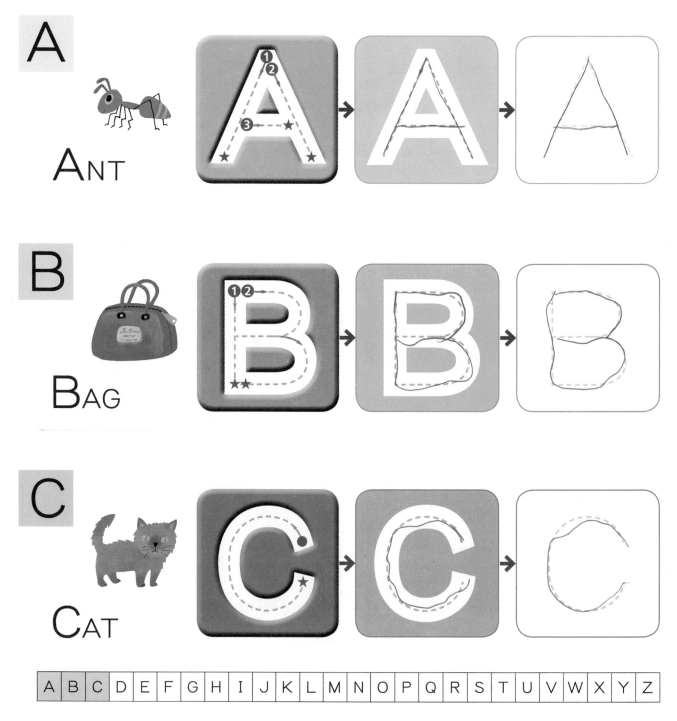

A B C D E F G H I J K L M N O P Q R S T U V W X Y Z

6

Counting Numbers 1 to 25

Level ★

Score

/100

Math
DAY
4

1 Draw a line from 1 to 25 in order while saying each number aloud.

100 points for completion

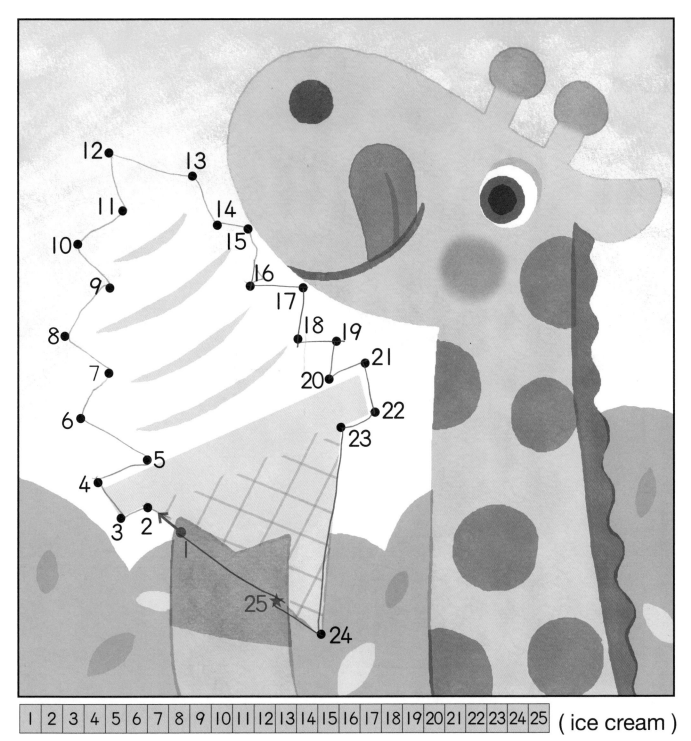

| 1 | 2 | 3 | 4 | 5 | 6 | 7 | 8 | 9 | 10 | 11 | 12 | 13 | 14 | 15 | 16 | 17 | 18 | 19 | 20 | 21 | 22 | 23 | 24 | 25 |

(ice cream)

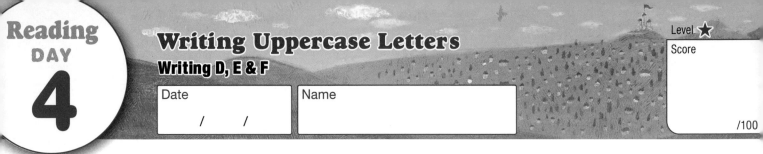

Date   /   /

Name

Level ★

Score

/100

① Say the name of each letter. Then say the sound of the letter as you trace it. Follow the stroke order indicated by the numbers.

100 points for comple

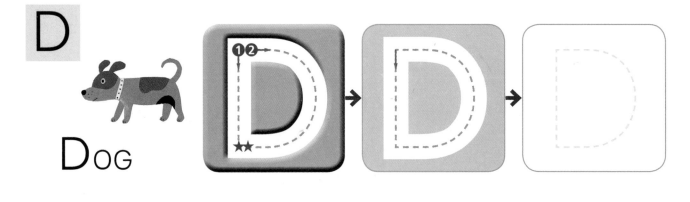

D
Dog

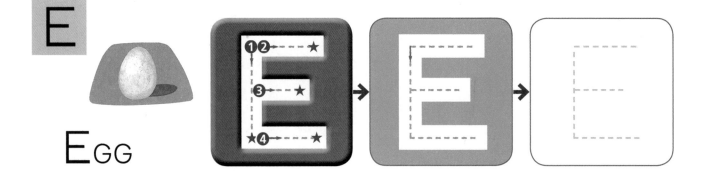

E
Egg

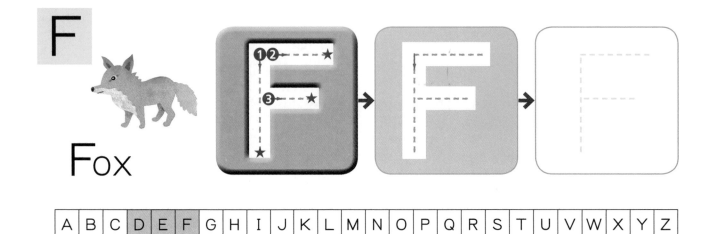

F
Fox

| A | B | C | D | E | F | G | H | I | J | K | L | M | N | O | P | Q | R | S | T | U | V | W | X | Y | Z |

Counting Numbers 1 to 30

Level ★
Score

/100

Math
DAY
5

Date / /

Name

1 Draw a line from 1 to 30 in order while saying each number aloud.

100 points for completion

| 1 | 2 | 3 | 4 | 5 | 6 | 7 | 8 | 9 | 10 | 11 | 12 | 13 | 14 | 15 | 16 | 17 | 18 | 19 | 20 | 21 | 22 | 23 | 24 | 25 | 26 | 27 | 28 | 29 | 30 |

9

(lion)

Writing Uppercase Letters
Writing G, H & I

Date / /

Name

Level ★

Score

/100

① Say the name of each letter. Then say the sound of the letter as you trace it. Follow the stroke order indicated by the numbers.

100 points for complete

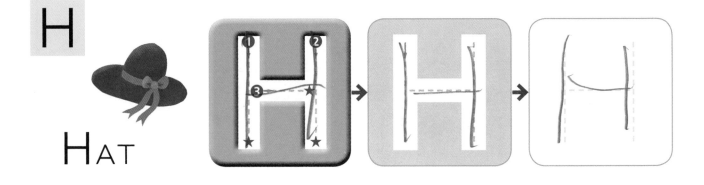

G — GIFT

H — HAT

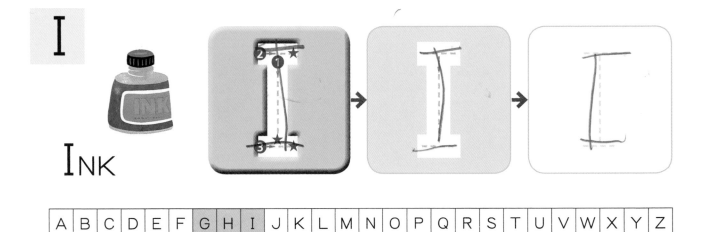

I — INK

| A | B | C | D | E | F | G | H | I | J | K | L | M | N | O | P | Q | R | S | T | U | V | W | X | Y | Z |

Writing Numbers 1 & 2

Level ★★

Score

/100

Math
DAY
6

Date   /   /

Name

1 Write the number and say it aloud.

50 points for completion

2 Write the number 2 and say it aloud.

50 points for completion

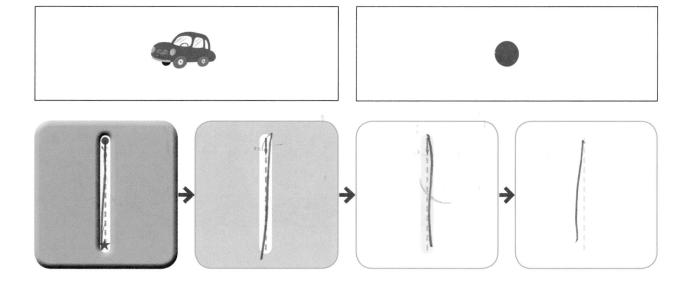

| 1 | 2 | 3 | 4 | 5 | 6 | 7 | 8 | 9 | 10 |

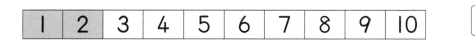
Your work is out of sight!

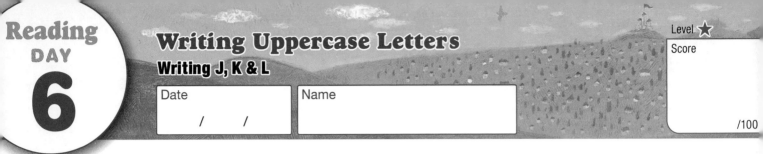

Reading DAY 6

Writing Uppercase Letters
Writing J, K & L

Date   /   /

Name

Level ⭐
Score

/100

① Say the name of each letter. Then say the sound of the letter as you trace it. Follow the stroke order indicated by the numbers.

100 points for compl

J

JAM

K

KEY

L

LION

| A | B | C | D | E | F | G | H | I | J | K | L | M | N | O | P | Q | R | S | T | U | V | W | X | Y | Z |

Writing Numbers 3 & 4

Level ★★

Score

/100

Date
7 / 4 / 12

Name

1 Write the number 3 and say it aloud.

50 points for completion

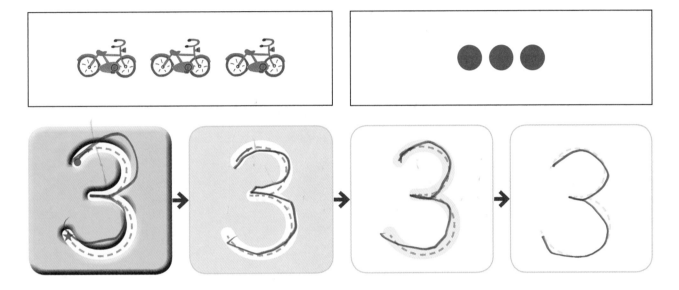

2 Write the number 4 and say it aloud.

50 points for completion

| 1 | 2 | 3 | 4 | 5 | 6 | 7 | 8 | 9 | 10 |

13

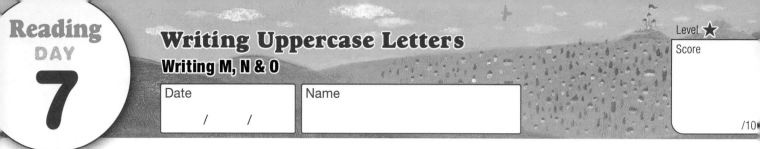

Reading
DAY
7

Writing Uppercase Letters
Writing M, N & O

Level ⭐
Score

/10

Date	Name
/ /	

① Say the name of each letter. Then say the sound of the letter as you trace it. Follow the stroke order indicated by the numbers.

100 points for cor

M

MAT

N

NUT

O

ORANGE

A	B	C	D	E	F	G	H	I	J	K	L	M	N	O	P	Q	R	S	T	U	V	W	X	Y	Z

Writing Numbers 5 & 6

Level ★★

Score

/100

Math DAY 8

Date / /

Name

1 Write the number 5 and say it aloud.

50 points for completion

2 Write the number 6 and say it aloud.

50 points for completion

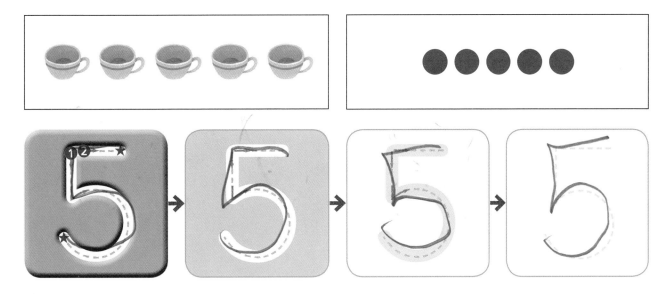

Writing Uppercase Letters
Writing P, Q & R

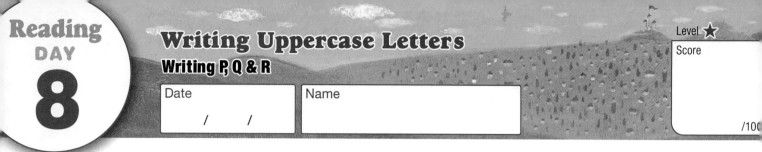

Date / /

Name

Level ★

Score

/100

① Say the name of each letter. Then say the sound of the letter as you trace it. Follow the stroke order indicated by the numbers.

100 points for comp

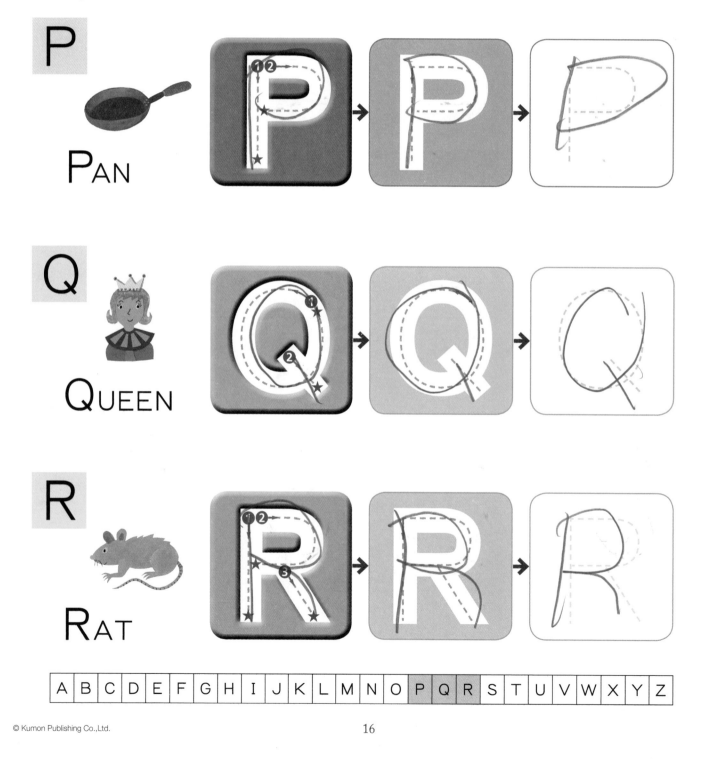

P

P<small>AN</small>

Q

Q<small>UEEN</small>

R

R<small>AT</small>

| A | B | C | D | E | F | G | H | I | J | K | L | M | N | O | P | Q | R | S | T | U | V | W | X | Y | Z |

Writing Numbers 7 & 8

Level ★★

Score

/100

Math
DAY
9

Date / /

Name

1 Write the number **7** and say it aloud.

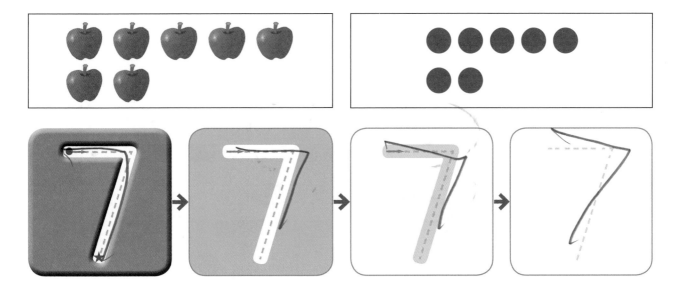

2 Write the number 8 and say it aloud.

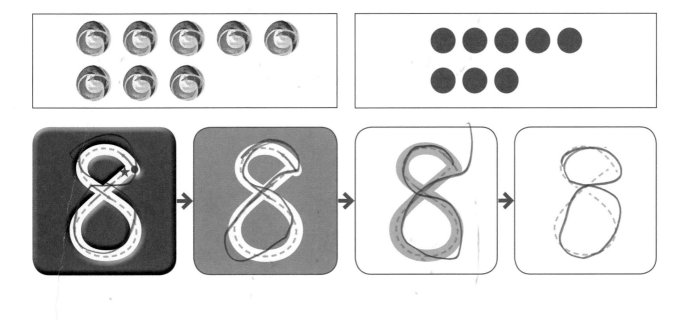

| 1 | 2 | 3 | 4 | 5 | 6 | 7 | 8 | 9 | 10 |

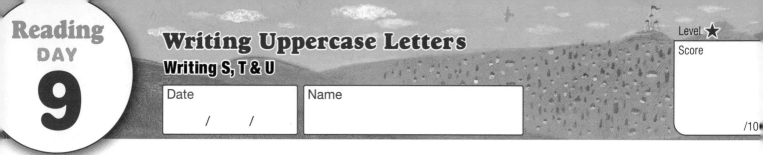

Writing Uppercase Letters
Writing S, T & U

Date / /   Name

Level ★
Score /10

① Say the name of each letter. Then say the sound of the letter as you trace it. Follow the stroke order indicated by the numbers.

100 points for com

S
SUN

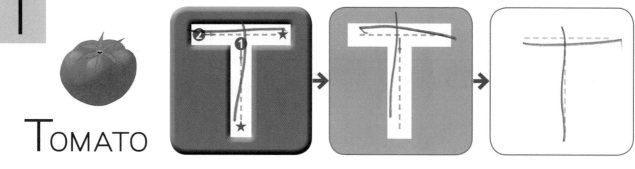

T
TOMATO

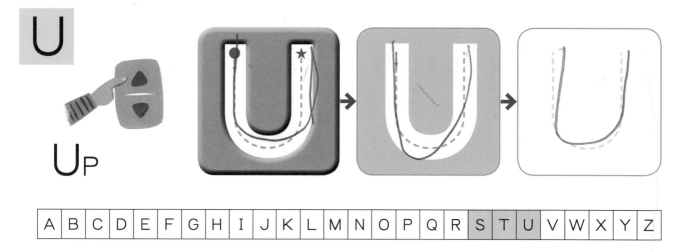

U
UP

A B C D E F G H I J K L M N O P Q R S T U V W X Y Z

Writing Numbers 9 & 10

Level ★★

Score

/100

Math
DAY
10

Date   /   /

Name

1 Write the number 9 and say it aloud.

50 points for completion

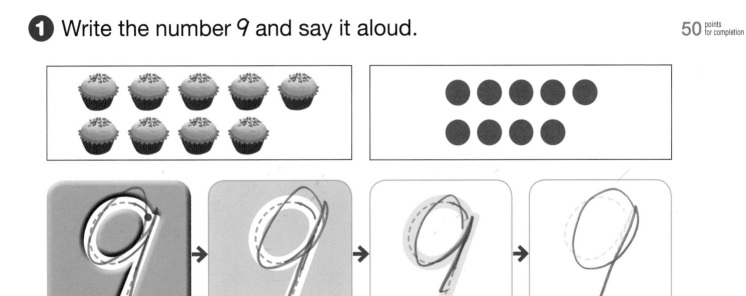

2 Write the number 10 and say it aloud.

50 points for completion

> If you want more numbers practice, check out Kumon's *My Book of NUMBERS 1-30*.

1	2	3	4	5	6	7	8	9	10

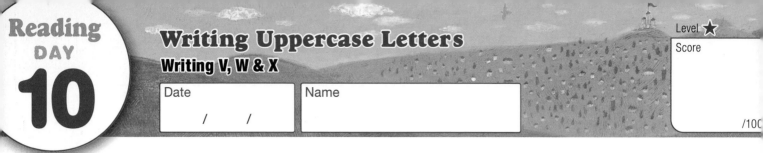

Reading DAY 10

Writing Uppercase Letters
Writing V, W & X

Level ★
Score

Date   /   /

Name

/100

① Say the name of each letter. Then say the sound of the letter as you trace it. Follow the stroke order indicated by the numbers.

100 points for comp

V

VAN

W

WATER

X

BOX

| A | B | C | D | E | F | G | H | I | J | K | L | M | N | O | P | Q | R | S | T | U | V | W | X | Y | Z |

Counting Numbers 1 to 30

Level ★★

Score

/100

Math
DAY
11

Date   /   /

Name

1 Trace the numbers 1 to 30. Then fill in the missing numbers. Say each number aloud.

100 points for completion

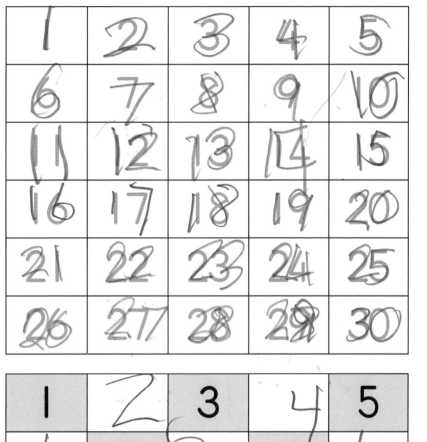

1	2	3	4	5
6	7	8	9	10
11	12	13	14	15
16	17	18	19	20
21	22	23	24	25
26	27	28	29	30

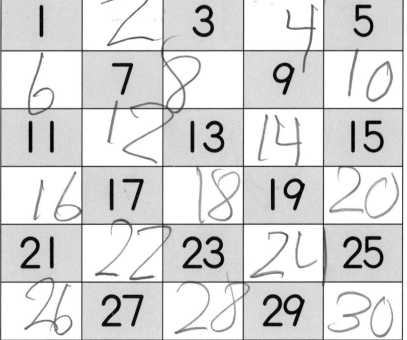

1	2	3	4	5
6	7	8	9	10
11	12	13	14	15
16	17	18	19	20
21	22	23	24	25
26	27	28	29	30

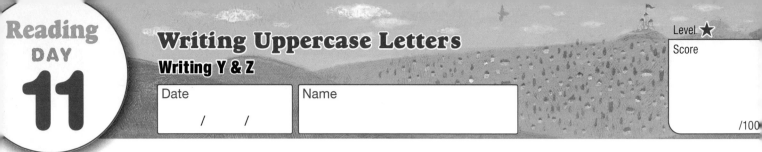

Reading DAY 11

Writing Uppercase Letters
Writing Y & Z

Level ★
Score

Date / /

Name

/100

① Say the name of each letter. Then say the sound of the letter as you trace it. Follow the stroke order indicated by the numbers.

100 points for compl

Y

YARD

Z

ZEBRA

Amazing work! Keep it up!

| A | B | C | D | E | F | G | H | I | J | K | L | M | N | O | P | Q | R | S | T | U | V | W | X | Y | Z |

Counting Numbers 1 to 40

Level ★★

Score

/100

Math
DAY
12

1 Fill in the missing numbers. Then trace the numbers 31 to 40. Say each number aloud.

100 points for completion

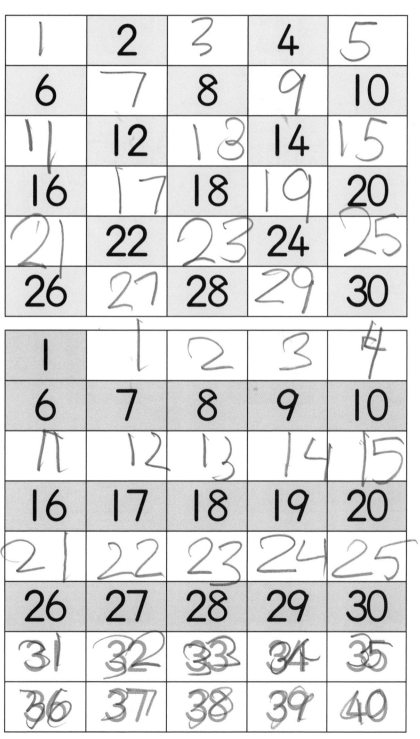

1	2	3	4	5
6	7	8	9	10
11	12	13	14	15
16	17	18	19	20
21	22	23	24	25
26	27	28	29	30

1	1	2	3	4
6	7	8	9	10
11	12	13	14	15
16	17	18	19	20
21	22	23	24	25
26	27	28	29	30
31	32	33	34	35
36	37	38	39	40

Reading DAY 12

Review
Writing A to Z

Date / /

Name

Level ⭐
Score

/100

① Trace the letters A to Z while saying each letter aloud.

100 points for compl

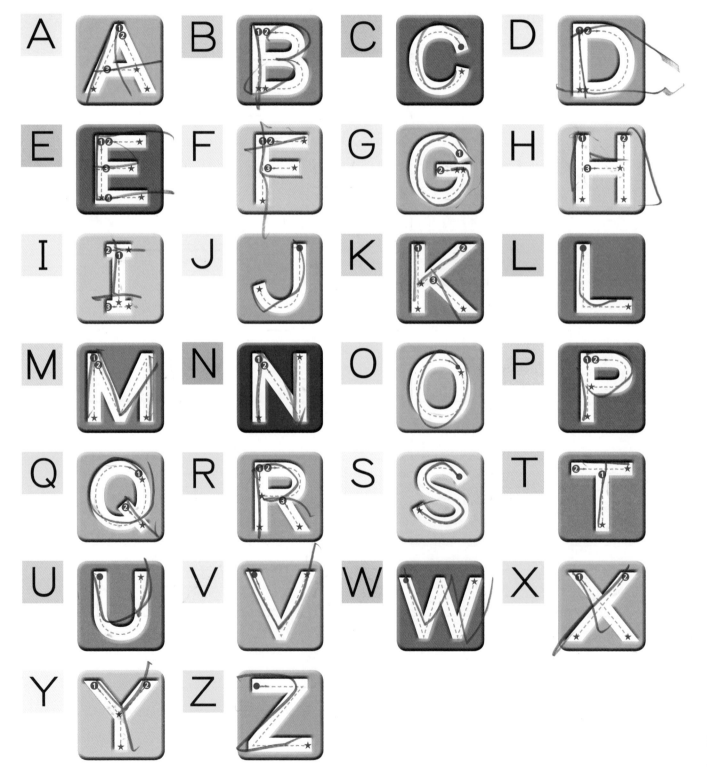

Counting Numbers 1 to 50

Level ★★

Score

/100

Math
DAY
13

Date   /   /

Name

1 Fill in the missing numbers. Then trace the numbers
41 to 50. Say each number aloud.

100 points for completion

1	2	3	4	5
6	7	8	9	10
11	12	13	14	15
16	17	18	19	20
21	22	23	24	25
26	27	28	29	30
31	32	33	34	35
36	37	38	39	40
41	42	43	44	45
46	47	48	49	50

Review
Writing A to Z

Level ★

Score

Date   /   /

Name

/100

① Trace the letters A to Z while saying each letter aloud.   100 points for compl

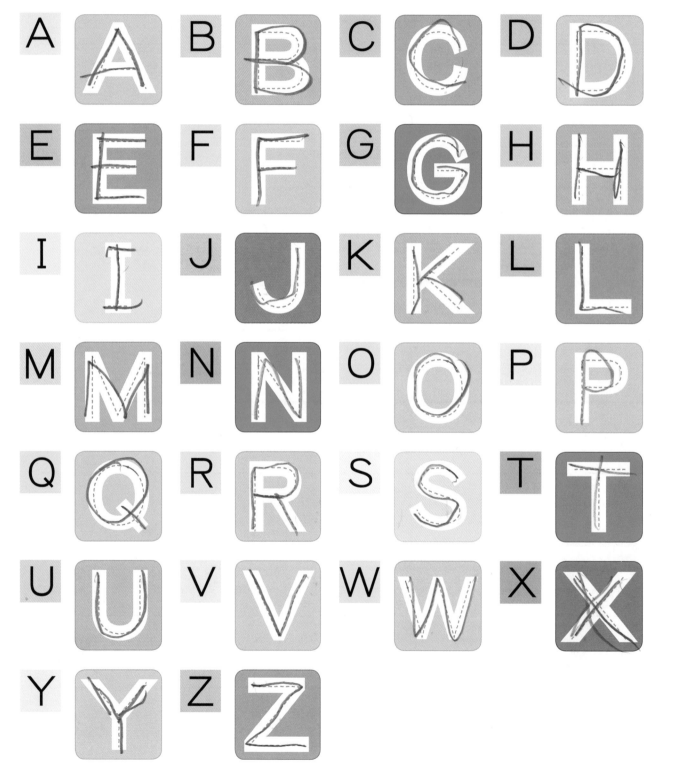

Counting Numbers 1 to 100

Level ★★

Score

/100

Math
DAY
14

Date
/ /

Name

1 Fill in the missing numbers. Then trace the numbers 51 to 100. Say each number aloud.

100 points for completion

1	2	3	4	5	6	7	8	9	10
11	12	13	14	15	16	17	18	19	20
21	22	23	24	25	26	27	28	29	30
31	32	33	34	35	36	37	38	39	40
41	42	43	44	45	46	47	48	49	50
51	52	53	54	55	56	57	58	59	60
61	62	63	64	65	66	67	68	69	70
71	72	73	74	75	76	77	78	79	80
81	82	83	84	85	86	87	88	89	90
91	92	93	94	95	96	97	98	99	100

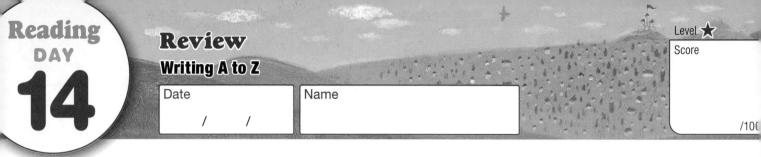

Review
Writing A to Z

Date   /   /   Name

Level ⭐
Score
/100

① Trace the letters A to Z while saying each letter aloud.   100 points for completion

A B C D

E F G H

I J K L

M N O P

Q R S T

U V W X

Y Z

You are a star!

Counting Numbers 1 to 110

Level ★★

Score

/100

Math
DAY
15

1 Fill in the missing numbers. Then trace the numbers
101 to 110. Say each number aloud.

100 points for completion

1	2	3	4	5	6	7	8	9	10
11	12	13	14	15	16	17	18	19	20
21	22	23	24	25	26	27	28	29	30
31	32	33	34	35	36	37	38	39	40
41	42	43	44	45	46	47	48	49	50
51	52	53	54	55	56	57	58	59	60
61	62	63	64	65	66	67	68	69	70
71	72	73	74	75	76	77	78	79	80
81	82	83	84	85	86	87	88	89	90
91	92	93	94	95	96	97	98	99	100
101	102	103	104	105	106	107	108	109	110

29

Lowercase Letters
"a" to "z"

Level ★
Score
/100

1 While saying each letter aloud, draw a line from a to z to connect the letters in alphabetical order.

100 points for comp

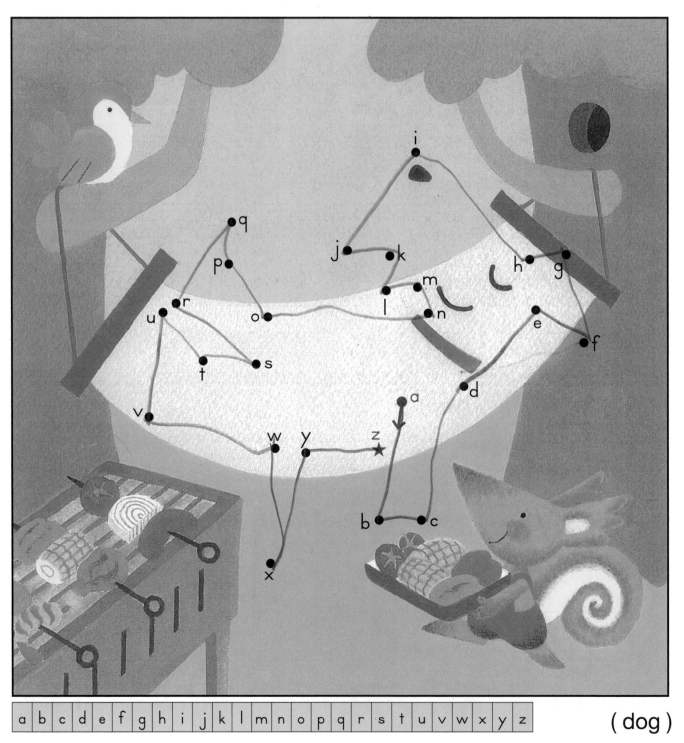

a b c d e f g h i j k l m n o p q r s t u v w x y z

(dog)

Counting Numbers 1 to 120

1 Fill in the missing numbers. Then trace the numbers 111 to 120. Say each number aloud.

100 points for completion

1	2	3	4	5	6	7	8	9	10
11	12	13	14	15	16	17	18	19	20
21	22	23	24	25	26	27	28	29	30
31	32	33	34	35	36	37	38	39	40
41	42	43	44	45	46	47	48	49	50
51	52	53	54	55	56	57	58	59	60
61	62	63	64	65	66	67	68	69	70
71	72	73	74	75	76	77	78	79	80
81	82	83	84	85	86	87	88	89	90
91	92	93	94	95	96	97	98	99	100
101	102	103	104	105	106	107	108	109	110
111	112	113	114	115	116	117	118	119	120

Lowercase Letters
"a" to "z"

Date   /   /

Name

① While saying each letter aloud, draw a line from a to z to connect the letters in alphabetical order.

100 points for completion

a b c d e f g h i j k l m n o p q r s t u v w x y z

(sea lion)

Counting Numbers 1 to 120

Level ★★

Score

Slaii

/100

Math DAY 17

Date / /

Name

1 Fill in the missing numbers. Say each number aloud.

100 points for completion

1	2	3	4	5	6	7	8	9	10
11	12	13	14	15	16	17	18	19	20
21	22	23	24	25	26	27	28	29	30
31	32	33	34	35	36	37	38	39	40
41	42	43	44	45	46	47	48	49	50
51	52	53	54	55	56	57	58	59	60
61	62	63	64	65	66	67	68	69	70
71	72	73	74	75	76	77	78	79	80
81	82	83	84	85	86	87	88	89	90
91	91	92	94	95	96	95	98	99	100
101	102	103	104	105	106	107	108	109	110
111	112	113	114	115	116	117	118	119	120

If you want more practice, check out Kumon's *My Book of NUMBERS 1-120*.

Writing Lowercase Letters
Writing a, b & c

Date / /

Name

Level ★

Score

/10

① Say the name of each letter. Then say the sound of the letter as you trace it. Follow the stroke order indicated by the numbers.

100 points for com

a

apple

b

bed

c

Cup

| a | b | c | d | e | f | g | h | i | j | k | l | m | n | o | p | q | r | s | t | u | v | w | x | y | z |

34

Level ★★

Math
DAY
18

Score

/100

Date   /   /

Name

1 Write the missing numbers.   10 points per question

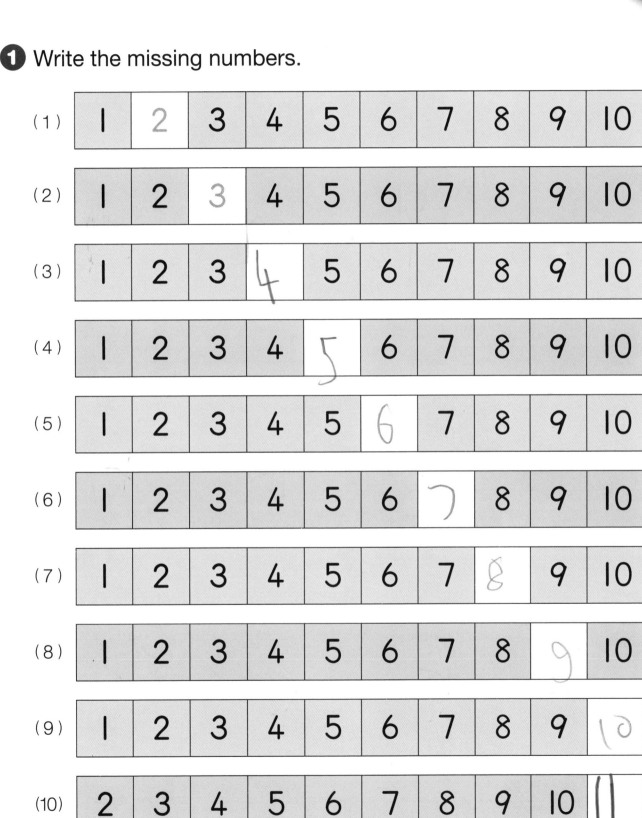

(1) 1 2 3 4 5 6 7 8 9 10

(2) 1 2 3 4 5 6 7 8 9 10

(3) 1 2 3 4 5 6 7 8 9 10

(4) 1 2 3 4 5 6 7 8 9 10

(5) 1 2 3 4 5 6 7 8 9 10

(6) 1 2 3 4 5 6 7 8 9 10

(7) 1 2 3 4 5 6 7 8 9 10

(8) 1 2 3 4 5 6 7 8 9 10

(9) 1 2 3 4 5 6 7 8 9 10

(10) 2 3 4 5 6 7 8 9 10 11

Reading
DAY
18

Writing Lowercase Letters
Writing d, e & f

Date / /

Name

Level ⭐
Score

/100

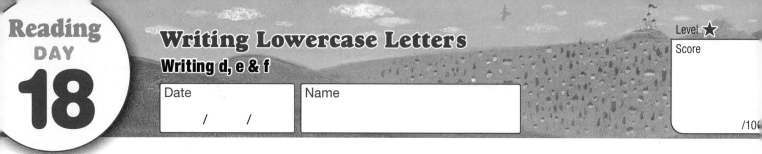

1 Say the name of each letter. Then say the sound of the letter as you trace it. Follow the stroke order indicated by the numbers.

100 points for comp

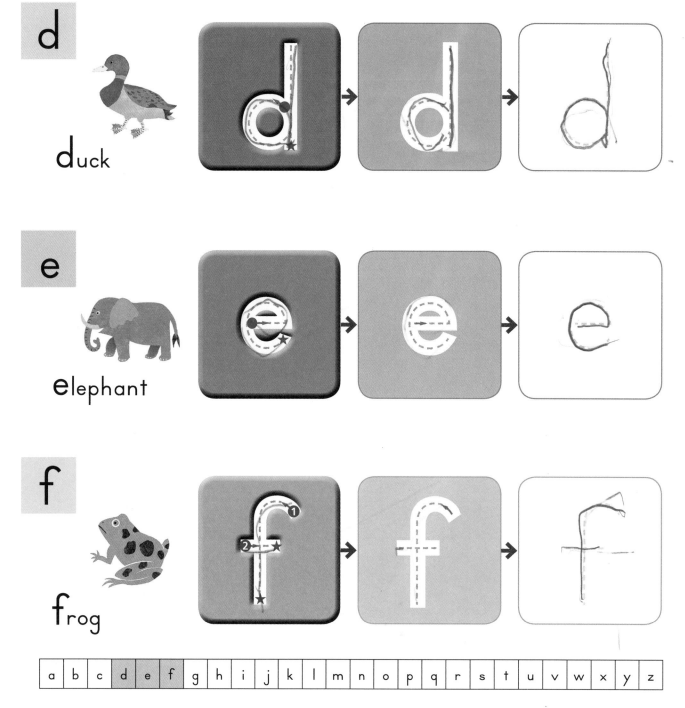

d

duck

e

elephant

f

frog

| a | b | c | d | e | f | g | h | i | j | k | l | m | n | o | p | q | r | s | t | u | v | w | x | y | z |

Adding 1

Date   /   /

Name

1 Read each number sentence aloud. Trace the answer in the number line. Then write the answer in the number sentence.

10 points per question

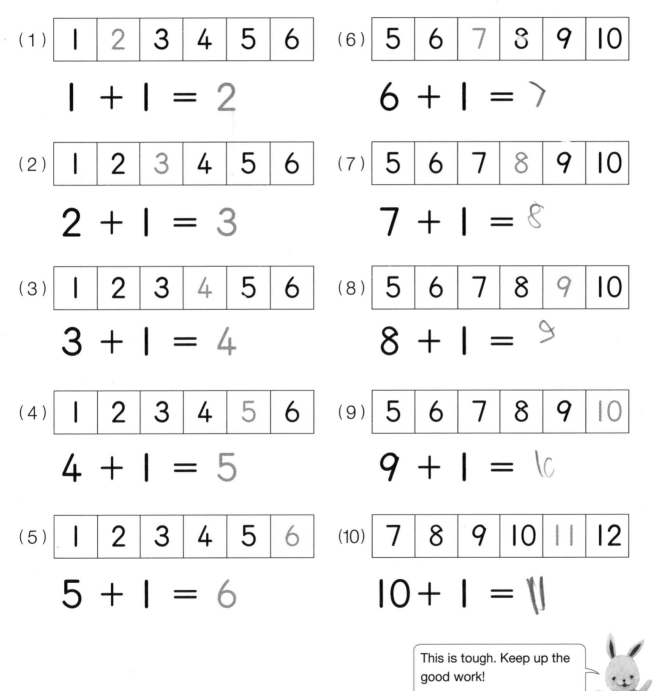

(1)

| 1 | 2 | 3 | 4 | 5 | 6 |

$1 + 1 = 2$

(2)

| 1 | 2 | 3 | 4 | 5 | 6 |

$2 + 1 = 3$

(3)

| 1 | 2 | 3 | 4 | 5 | 6 |

$3 + 1 = 4$

(4)

| 1 | 2 | 3 | 4 | 5 | 6 |

$4 + 1 = 5$

(5)

| 1 | 2 | 3 | 4 | 5 | 6 |

$5 + 1 = 6$

(6)

| 5 | 6 | 7 | 8 | 9 | 10 |

$6 + 1 = 7$

(7)

| 5 | 6 | 7 | 8 | 9 | 10 |

$7 + 1 = 8$

(8)

| 5 | 6 | 7 | 8 | 9 | 10 |

$8 + 1 = 9$

(9)

| 5 | 6 | 7 | 8 | 9 | 10 |

$9 + 1 = 10$

(10)

| 7 | 8 | 9 | 10 | 11 | 12 |

$10 + 1 = 11$

This is tough. Keep up the good work!

Writing Lowercase Letters
Writing g, h & i

Level ★
Score

Date
/   /

Name

/100

① Say the name of each letter. Then say the sound of the letter as you trace it. Follow the stroke order indicated by the numbers.

100 points for com

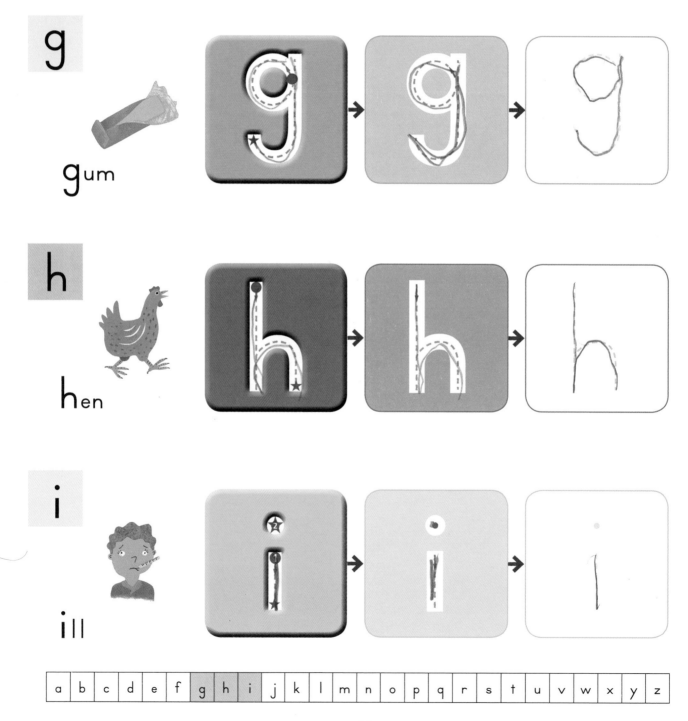

g

gum

h

hen

i

ill

| a | b | c | d | e | f | g | h | i | j | k | l | m | n | o | p | q | r | s | t | u | v | w | x | y | z |

Adding 1

Level ★★★
Score

/100

Math
DAY
20

1 Add the numbers. Use the number line as a guide.

5 points per question

| 1 | 2 | 3 | 4 | 5 | 6 | 7 | 8 | 9 | 10 | 11 | 12 | 13 | 14 | 15 |

(1) $1 + 1 = 2$

(2) $2 + 1 = 3$

(3) $3 + 1 = 4$

(4) $4 + 1 = 5$

(5) $5 + 1 = 6$

(6) $6 + 1 = 7$

(7) $7 + 1 = 8$

(8) $8 + 1 = 9$

(9) $9 + 1 = 10$

(10) $10 + 1 = 11$

2 Add.

5 points per question

(1) $4 + 1 = 5$

(2) $5 + 1 = 6$

(3) $1 + 1 = 2$

(4) $2 + 1 = 3$

(5) $8 + 1 = 9$

(6) $3 + 1 = 4$

(7) $6 + 1 = 7$

(8) $7 + 1 = 8$

(9) $9 + 1 = 10$

(10) $10 + 1 = 11$

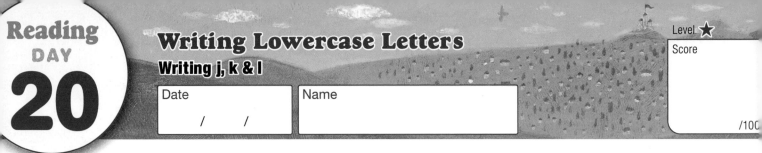

Reading
DAY
20

Writing Lowercase Letters
Writing j, k & l

Date   /   /

Name

Level ⭐

Score

/100

① Say the name of each letter. Then say the sound of the letter as you trace it. Follow the stroke order indicated by the numbers.

100 points for comp

Adding 2

Level ★★

Score

/100

Math
DAY
21

Date   /   /

Name

1 Write the missing numbers.

10 points per question

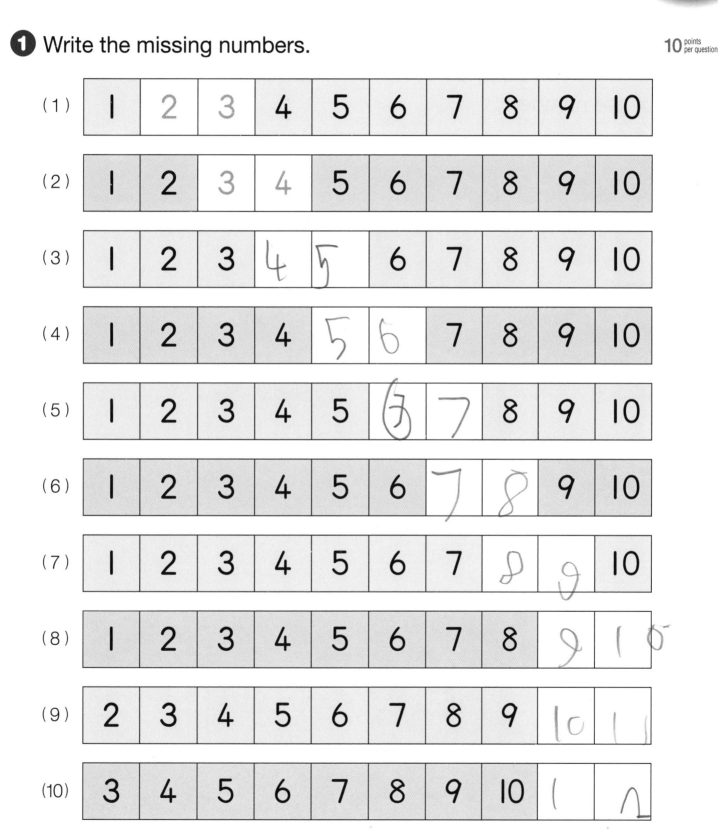

(1) 1 2 3 4 5 6 7 8 9 10

(2) 1 2 3 4 5 6 7 8 9 10

(3) 1 2 3 4 5 6 7 8 9 10

(4) 1 2 3 4 5 6 7 8 9 10

(5) 1 2 3 4 5 6 7 8 9 10

(6) 1 2 3 4 5 6 7 8 9 10

(7) 1 2 3 4 5 6 7 8 9 10

(8) 1 2 3 4 5 6 7 8 9 10

(9) 2 3 4 5 6 7 8 9 10 11

(10) 3 4 5 6 7 8 9 10 11 12

Writing Lowercase Letters
Writing m, n & o

Date / /

Name

① Say the name of each letter. Then say the sound of the letter as you trace it. Follow the stroke order indicated by the numbers.

100 points for comp

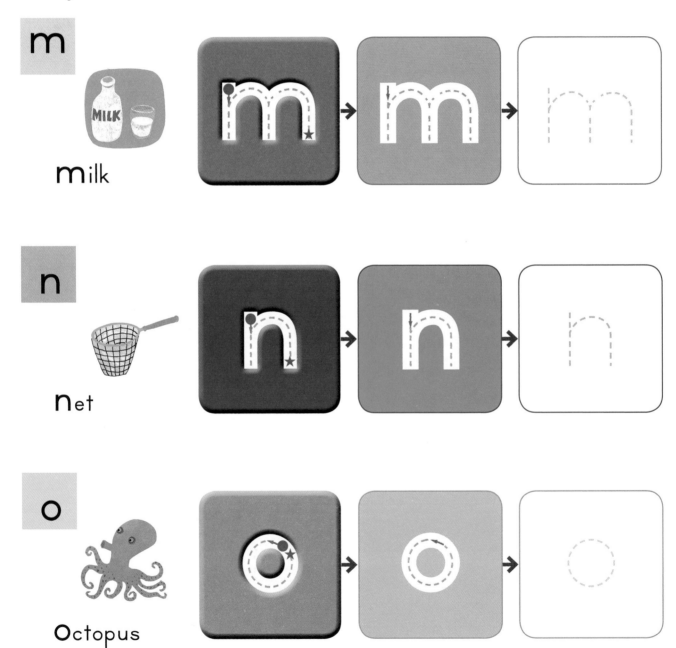

m

milk

n

net

o

Octopus

| a | b | c | d | e | f | g | h | i | j | k | l | m | n | o | p | q | r | s | t | u | v | w | x | y | z |

Adding 2

Level ★★★
Score

/100

Math
DAY
22

1 Read each number sentence aloud. Trace the answer in the number line. Then write the answer in the number sentence.

10 points per question

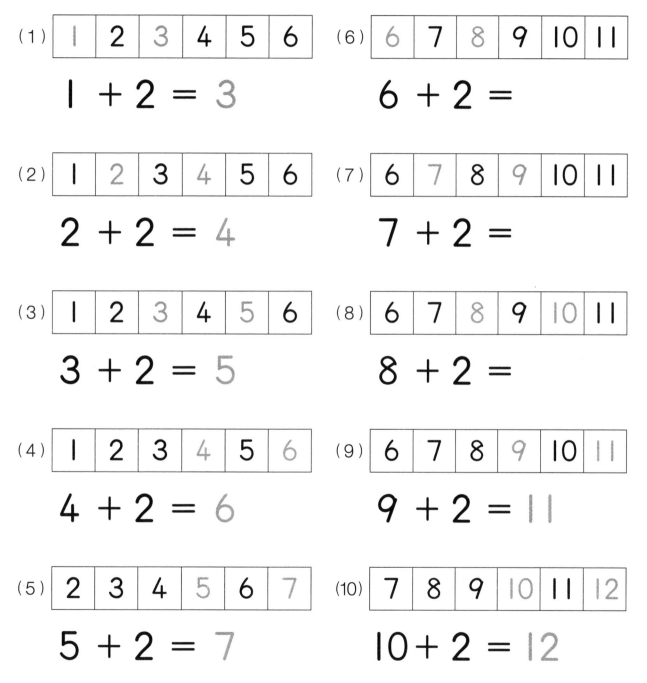

(1)

| 1 | 2 | 3 | 4 | 5 | 6 |

$$1 + 2 = 3$$

(2)

| 1 | 2 | 3 | 4 | 5 | 6 |

$$2 + 2 = 4$$

(3)

| 1 | 2 | 3 | 4 | 5 | 6 |

$$3 + 2 = 5$$

(4)

| 1 | 2 | 3 | 4 | 5 | 6 |

$$4 + 2 = 6$$

(5)

| 2 | 3 | 4 | 5 | 6 | 7 |

$$5 + 2 = 7$$

(6)

| 6 | 7 | 8 | 9 | 10 | 11 |

$$6 + 2 =$$

(7)

| 6 | 7 | 8 | 9 | 10 | 11 |

$$7 + 2 =$$

(8)

| 6 | 7 | 8 | 9 | 10 | 11 |

$$8 + 2 =$$

(9)

| 6 | 7 | 8 | 9 | 10 | 11 |

$$9 + 2 = 11$$

(10)

| 7 | 8 | 9 | 10 | 11 | 12 |

$$10 + 2 = 12$$

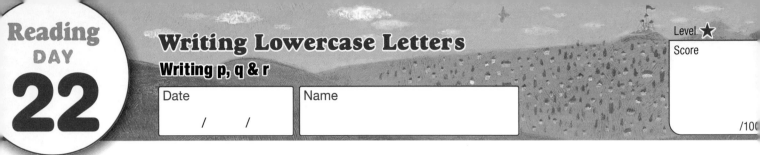

Writing Lowercase Letters
Writing p, q & r

Date   /   /

Name

Level ★

Score

/100

① Say the name of each letter. Then say the sound of the letter as you trace it. Follow the stroke order indicated by the numbers.

100 points for comp

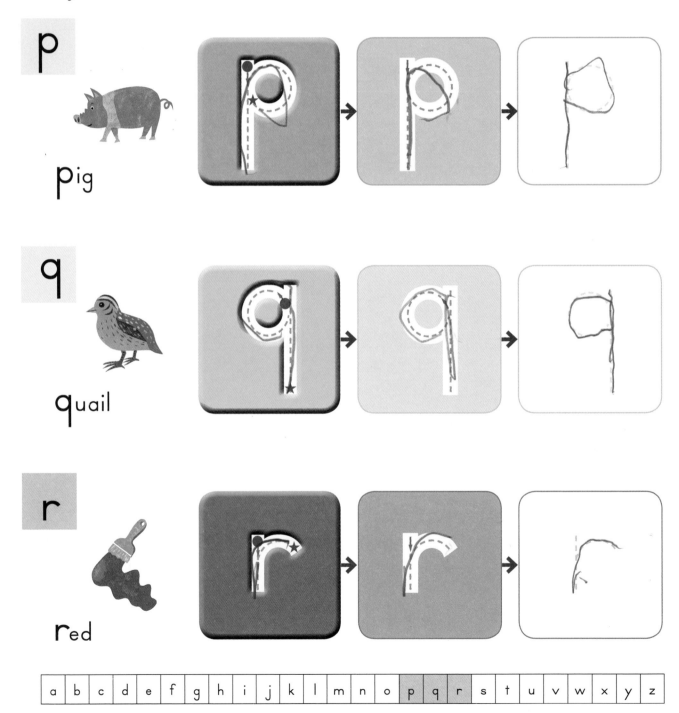

Adding 2

Level ★★★

Score

/100

Math
DAY
23

Date
/ /

Name

1 Add the numbers. Use the number line as a guide.

5 points per question

| 1 | 2 | 3 | 4 | 5 | 6 | 7 | 8 | 9 | 10 | 11 | 12 | 13 | 14 | 15 |

(1) 1 + 2 = 3

(2) 2 + 2 = 4

(3) 3 + 2 = 5

(4) 4 + 2 = 6

(5) 5 + 2 = 7

(6) 6 + 2 = 8

(7) 7 + 2 = 9

(8) 8 + 2 = 10

(9) 9 + 2 = 11

(10) 10 + 2 = 12

2 Add.

5 points per question

(1) 1 + 2 = 3

(2) 5 + 2 = 7

(3) 6 + 2 = 8

(4) 3 + 2 = 5

(5) 4 + 2 = 6

(6) 7 + 2 = 9

(7) 8 + 2 = 10

(8) 2 + 2 = 4

(9) 9 + 2 = 11

(10) 10 + 2 = 12

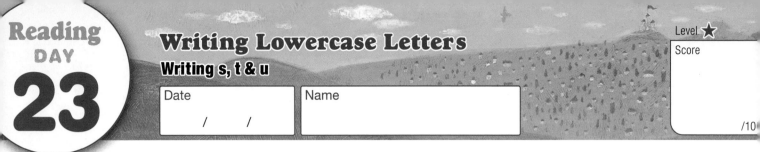

Writing Lowercase Letters

Writing s, t & u

Level ★

Score

/10

Date   /   /

Name

① Say the name of each letter. Then say the sound of the letter as you trace it. Follow the stroke order indicated by the numbers.

100 points for com

s

Sand

t

tent

u

Umbrella

| a | b | c | d | e | f | g | h | i | j | k | l | m | n | o | p | q | r | s | t | u | v | w | x | y | z |

© Kumon Publishing Co.,Ltd.

46

Review
Addition

Date / /

Name

Level ★★★

Score

/100

Math
DAY
24

1 Add the numbers.

5 points per question

(1) $3 + 1 = 4$

(2) $5 + 2 = 7$

(3) $8 + 1 = 9$

(4) $6 + 1 = 7$

(5) $4 + 2 = 6$

(6) $7 + 1 = 8$

(7) $5 + 1 = 6$

(8) $8 + 2 = 10$

(9) $1 + 2 = 3$

(10) $9 + 1 = 10$

(11) $6 + 2 = 8$

(12) $10 + 1 = 11$

(13) $2 + 1 = 3$

(14) $3 + 2 = 5$

(15) $2 + 2 = 4$

(16) $4 + 1 = 5$

(17) $1 + 1 = 2$

(18) $7 + 2 = 9$

(19) $9 + 2 = 11$

(20) $10 + 2 = 12$

Wow! You've got it now!

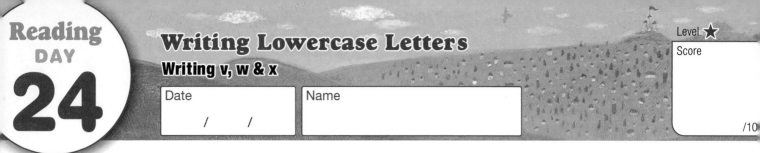

Reading
DAY
24

Writing Lowercase Letters
Writing v, w & x

Date   /   /

Name

Level ★
Score

/10

① Say the name of each letter. Then say the sound of the letter as you trace it. Follow the stroke order indicated by the numbers.

100 points for com

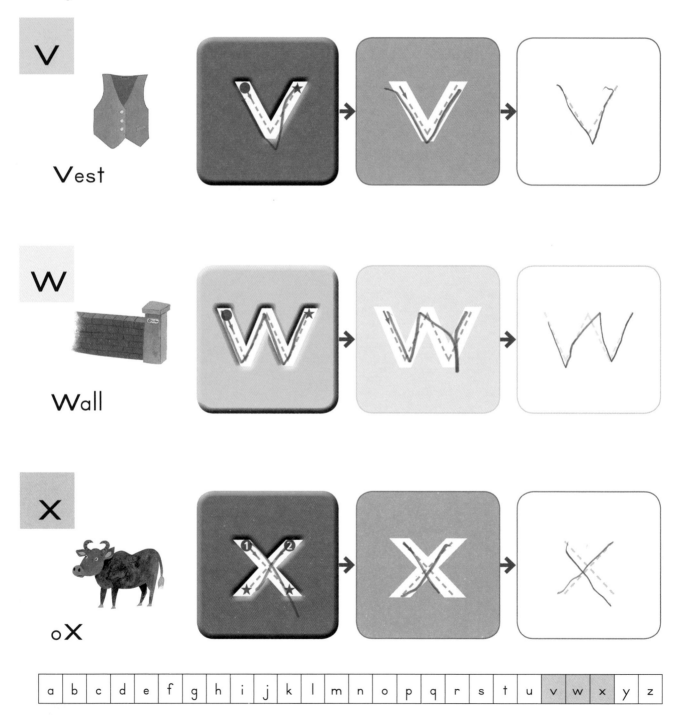

v

Vest

w

Wall

x

oX

| a | b | c | d | e | f | g | h | i | j | k | l | m | n | o | p | q | r | s | t | u | v | w | x | y | z |

Subtracting 1

Level ★★★

Score /100

Name

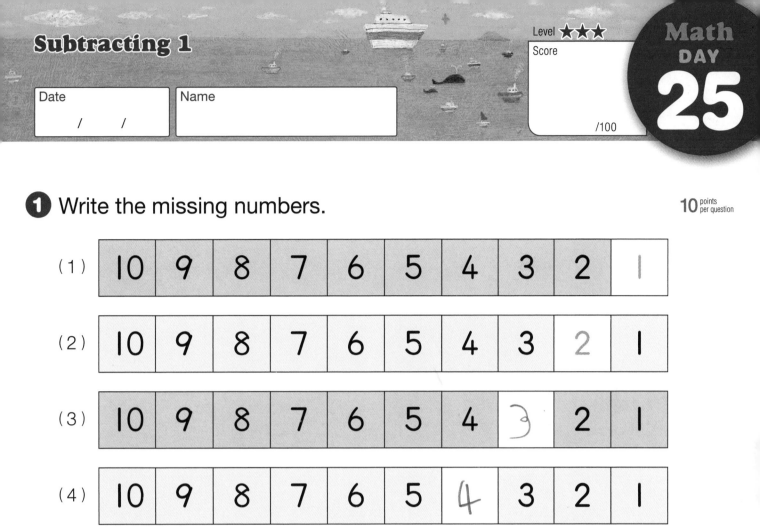

1 Write the missing numbers.   **10** points per question

(1) 10 9 8 7 6 5 4 3 2 1

(2) 10 9 8 7 6 5 4 3 2 1

(3) 10 9 8 7 6 5 4 3 2 1

(4) 10 9 8 7 6 5 4 3 2 1

(5) 10 9 8 7 6 5 4 3 2 1

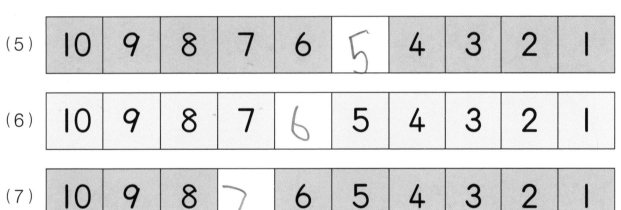

(6) 10 9 8 7 6 5 4 3 2 1

(7) 10 9 8 7 6 5 4 3 2 1

(8) 10 9 8 7 6 5 4 3 2 1

(9) 10 9 8 7 6 5 4 3 2 1

(10) 11 10 9 8 7 6 5 4 3 2

© Kumon Publishing Co.,Ltd.

49

Writing Lowercase Letters
Writing y & z

Date   /   /

Name

① Say the name of each letter. Then say the sound of the letter as you trace it. Follow the stroke order indicated by the numbers.

100 points for com

y-o-yo

z-oo

Great job! You're a champ!

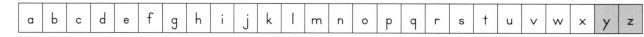

a b c d e f g h i j k l m n o p q r s t u v w x y z

Subtracting 1

Level ★★★

Score

End

/100

Math
DAY
26

Date / /

Name

1 Read each number sentence aloud. Trace the answer in the number line. Then write the answer in the number sentence. 10 points per question

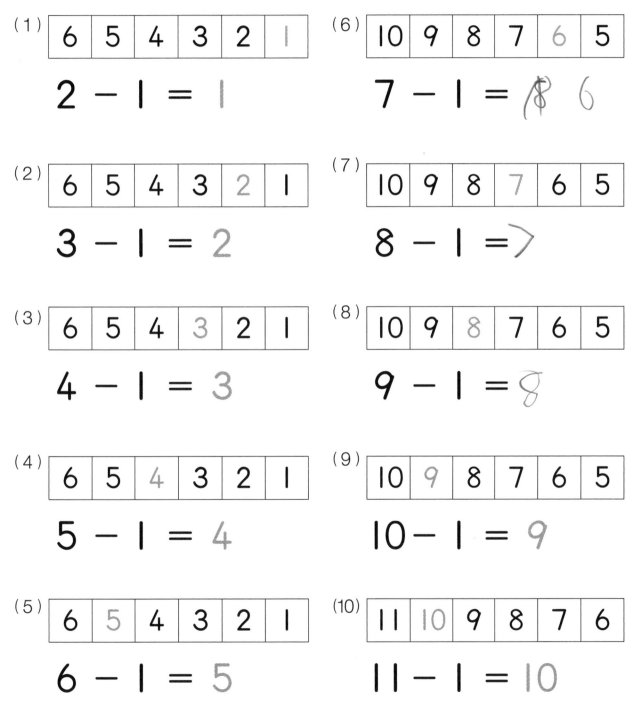

(1)

| 6 | 5 | 4 | 3 | 2 | 1 |

2 – 1 = 1

(2)

| 6 | 5 | 4 | 3 | 2 | 1 |

3 – 1 = 2

(3)

| 6 | 5 | 4 | 3 | 2 | 1 |

4 – 1 = 3

(4)

| 6 | 5 | 4 | 3 | 2 | 1 |

5 – 1 = 4

(5)

| 6 | 5 | 4 | 3 | 2 | 1 |

6 – 1 = 5

(6)

| 10 | 9 | 8 | 7 | 6 | 5 |

7 – 1 = 6

(7)

| 10 | 9 | 8 | 7 | 6 | 5 |

8 – 1 = 7

(8)

| 10 | 9 | 8 | 7 | 6 | 5 |

9 – 1 = 8

(9)

| 10 | 9 | 8 | 7 | 6 | 5 |

10 – 1 = 9

(10)

| 11 | 10 | 9 | 8 | 7 | 6 |

11 – 1 = 10

Review
Writing a to z

Date   /   /

Name

Level ⭐

Score

/10

① Trace the letters "a" to "z" while saying each letter aloud.

100 points for comp

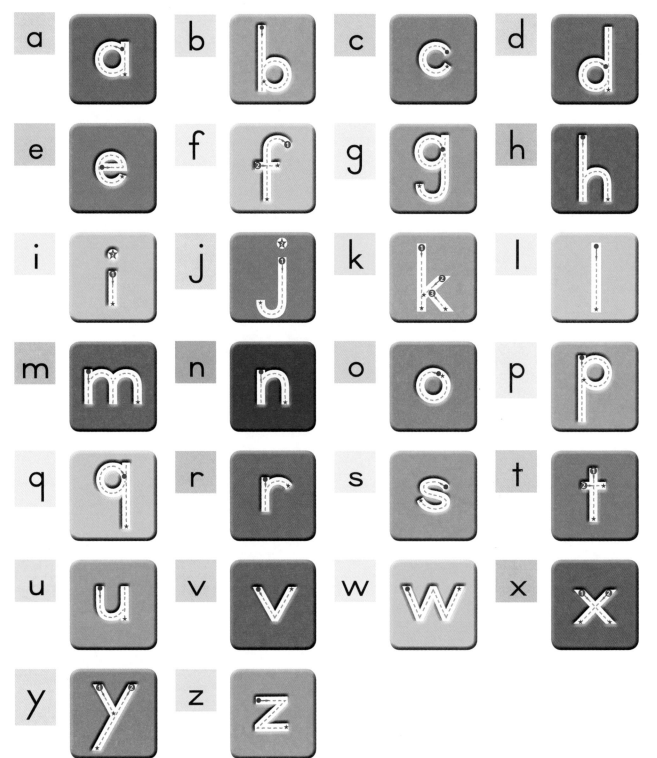

52

❶ Subtract the numbers. Use the number line as a guide.   5 points per question

| 15 | 14 | 13 | 12 | 11 | 10 | 9 | 8 | 7 | 6 | 5 | 4 | 3 | 2 | 1 |

(1) 2 − 1 = 1

(2) 3 − 1 =

(3) 4 − 1 =

(4) 5 − 1 =

(5) 6 − 1 =

(6) 7 − 1 =

(7) 8 − 1 =

(8) 9 − 1 =

(9) 10 − 1 = 9

(10) 11 − 1 = 10

❷ Subtract.   5 points per question

(1) 5 − 1 =

(2) 3 − 1 =

(3) 6 − 1 =

(4) 7 − 1 =

(5) 9 − 1 =

(6) 8 − 1 =

(7) 4 − 1 =

(8) 10 − 1 =

(9) 2 − 1 =

(10) 11 − 1 =

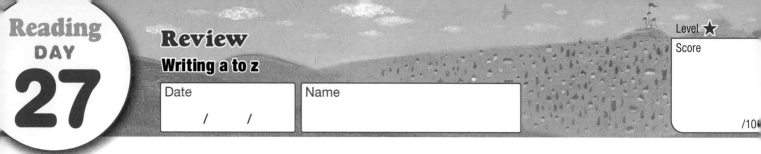

Reading
DAY
27

Review
Writing a to z

Date   /   /

Name

Level ★

Score

/100

① Trace the letters "a" to "z" while saying each letter aloud.   100 points for completion

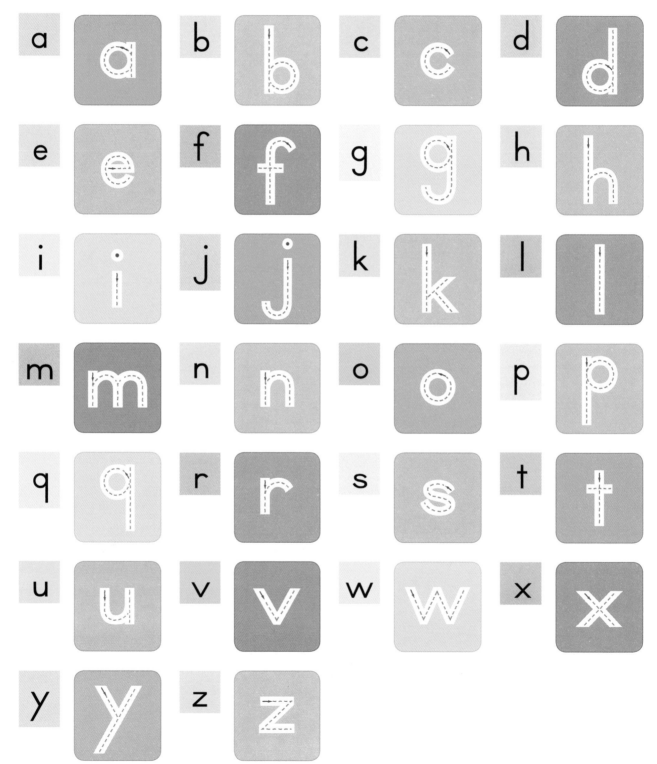

Level ★★★

Score

/100

Date   /   /

Name

1 Trace the numbers in each number line. Then write the missing numbers.   10 points per question

(1) | 10 | 9 | 8 | 7 | 6 | 5 | 4 | 3 | 2 | 1 |

(2) | 10 | 9 | 8 | 7 | 6 | 5 | 4 | 3 | 2 | 1 |

(3) | 10 | 9 | 8 | 7 | 6 | 5 | | | 2 | 1 |

(4) | 10 | 9 | 8 | 7 | 6 | | | 3 | 2 | 1 |

(5) | 10 | 9 | 8 | 7 | | | 4 | 3 | 2 | 1 |

(6) | 10 | 9 | 8 | | | 5 | 4 | 3 | 2 | 1 |

(7) | 10 | 9 | | | 6 | 5 | 4 | 3 | 2 | 1 |

(8) | 10 | | | 7 | 6 | 5 | 4 | 3 | 2 | 1 |

(9) | 11 | | | 8 | 7 | 6 | 5 | 4 | 3 | 2 |

(10) | 12 | | | 9 | 8 | 7 | 6 | 5 | 4 | 3 |

Reading
DAY
28

Review
Writing a to z

Date
/ /

Name

Level ★
Score

/100

1 Trace the letters "a" to "z" while saying each letter aloud.   **100** points for comple

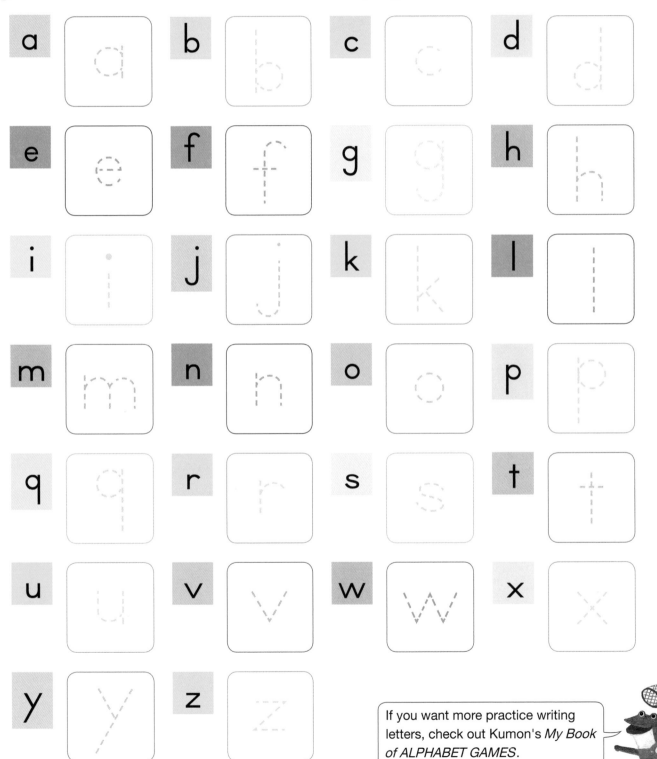

If you want more practice writing letters, check out Kumon's *My Book of ALPHABET GAMES*.

Date   /   /

Name

1 Read each number sentence aloud. Trace the answer in the 10 points per question
number line. Then write the answer in the number sentence.

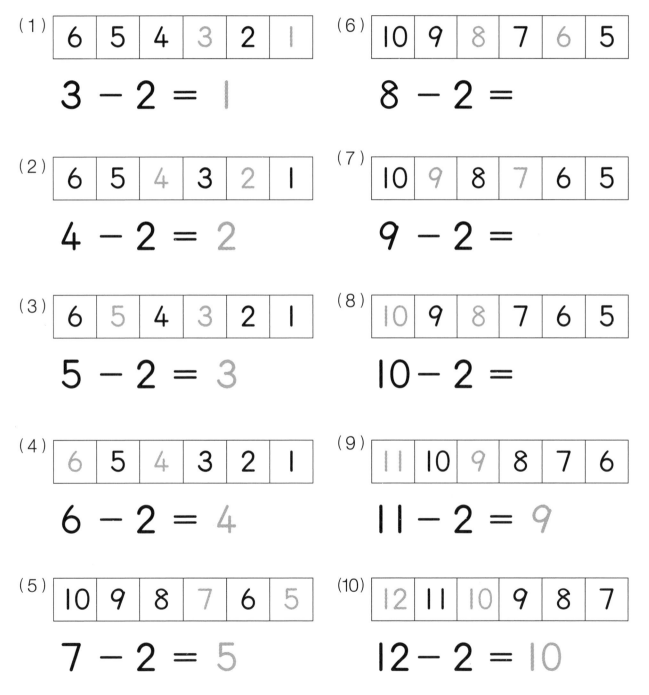

(1)

6	5	4	3	2	1

$3 - 2 = 1$

(2)

6	5	4	3	2	1

$4 - 2 = 2$

(3)

6	5	4	3	2	1

$5 - 2 = 3$

(4)

6	5	4	3	2	1

$6 - 2 = 4$

(5)

10	9	8	7	6	5

$7 - 2 = 5$

(6)

10	9	8	7	6	5

$8 - 2 =$

(7)

10	9	8	7	6	5

$9 - 2 =$

(8)

10	9	8	7	6	5

$10 - 2 =$

(9)

11	10	9	8	7	6

$11 - 2 = 9$

(10)

12	11	10	9	8	7

$12 - 2 = 10$

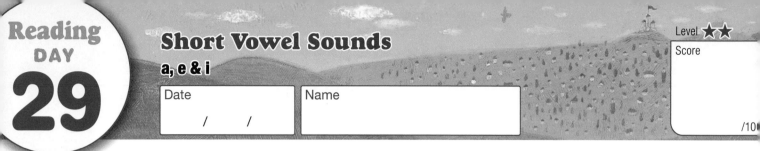

Reading
DAY
29

Short Vowel Sounds
a, e & i

Level ★★
Score

/100

Date
/ /

Name

① Trace or write the correct vowels to finish each rhyming pair of words below. **10** points per question

(1)   c a t   h __ t

(2)   m __ n   p __ n

(3)   d __ d   m __ d

(4)   b __ g   t __ g

(5)   p e n   m __ n

(6)   j __ t   p __ t

② Connect each word to the correct picture below. **40** points for comp

(1) leg •

(2) bed •

(3) hit •

(4) rip •

(5) pin •

(6) pig •

• ⓐ

• ⓑ

• ⓒ

• ⓓ

• ⓔ

• ⓕ

Date
/ /

Name

1 Subtract the numbers. Use the number line as a guide.   5 points per question

15	14	13	12	11	10	9	8	7	6	5	4	3	2	1

(1) $3 - 2 = 1$

(2) $4 - 2 =$

(3) $5 - 2 =$

(4) $6 - 2 =$

(5) $7 - 2 =$

(6) $8 - 2 =$

(7) $9 - 2 =$

(8) $10 - 2 = 8$

(9) $11 - 2 = 9$

(10) $12 - 2 = 10$

2 Subtract.   5 points per question

(1) $5 - 2 =$

(2) $3 - 2 =$

(3) $6 - 2 =$

(4) $7 - 2 =$

(5) $9 - 2 =$

(6) $8 - 2 =$

(7) $4 - 2 =$

(8) $10 - 2 =$

(9) $12 - 2 =$

(10) $11 - 2 =$

Reading
DAY
30

Short Vowel Sounds
i, o & u

Level ★★
Score

Date   /   /

Name

/100

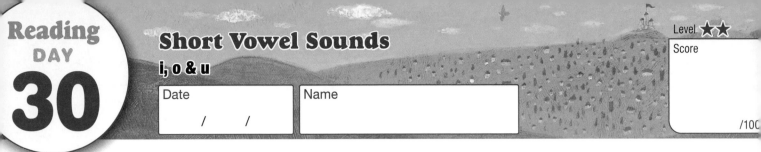

① Trace or write the correct vowels to finish each rhyming pair of words below.   **10** points per question

(1)   k_i_d   l__d

(2)   l o g   h__g

(3)   d__t   h__t

(4)   f__x   b__x

(5)   r__b   j__b

(6)   h__p   m__p

② Connect each word to the correct picture below.   **40** points for compl

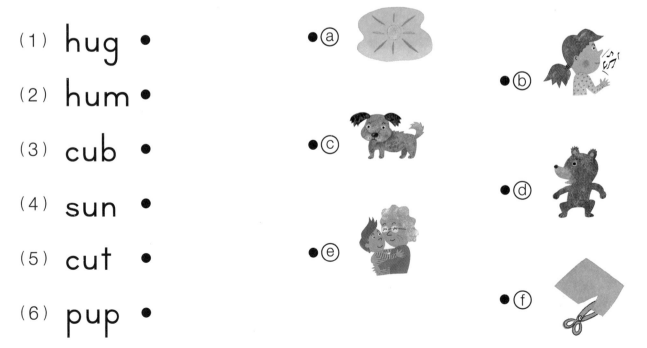

(1) hug •

(2) hum •

(3) cub •

(4) sun •

(5) cut •

(6) pup •

•ⓐ

•ⓑ

•ⓒ

•ⓓ

•ⓔ

•ⓕ

Review
Subtraction

Date
/   /

Name

Level ★★★
Score

/100

Math
DAY
31

1 Subtract.

5 points per question

(1) $3 - 1 =$

(2) $5 - 2 =$

(3) $8 - 1 =$

(4) $6 - 1 =$

(5) $4 - 2 =$

(6) $7 - 1 =$

(7) $5 - 1 =$

(8) $8 - 2 =$

(9) $11 - 2 =$

(10) $9 - 1 =$

(11) $6 - 2 =$

(12) $10 - 1 =$

(13) $2 - 1 =$

(14) $3 - 2 =$

(15) $12 - 2 =$

(16) $4 - 1 =$

(17) $11 - 1 =$

(18) $7 - 2 =$

(19) $9 - 2 =$

(20) $10 - 2 =$

If you want more subtraction practice, check out Kumon's *My Book of SIMPLE SUBTRACTION*.

Short Vowel Sounds
a, e, i, o & u

Date   /   /

Name

① Write the correct vowels to finish each rhyming pair of words below.

50 points for comp

(1)

	p	
b	e	g
	g	

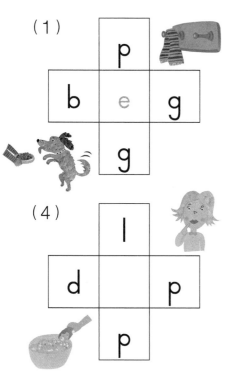

(2)

	m	
f		x
	x	

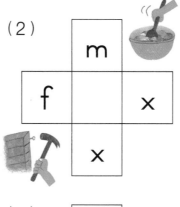

(3)

	s	
p		t
	t	

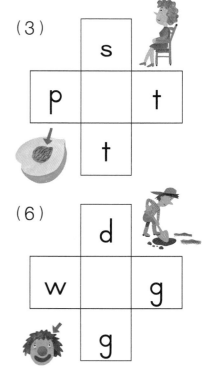

(4)

	l	
d		p
	p	

(5)

	f	
b		n
	n	

(6)

	d	
w		g
	g	

② Trace the word below each picture.

50 points for comp

(1)   _ox_

(2)   _sob_

(3)   _top_

(4)   _rag_

(5)   _hen_

(6)   _wet_

(7)   _hid_

(8)   _fog_

(9)   _pot_

(10)   _bug_

(11)   _gum_

(12)   _tub_

Telling Time

Level ★★★

Score

/100

Math
DAY
32

Date / /

Name

1 What time is it? Write the time under each clock.

5 points per question

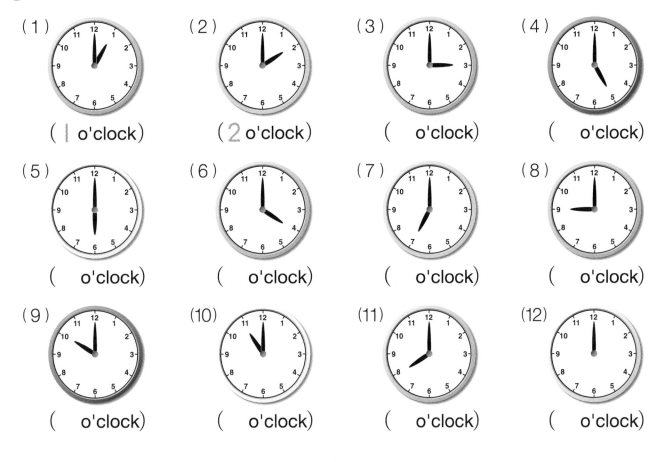

(1) (| o'clock)

(2) (2 o'clock)

(3) (o'clock)

(4) (o'clock)

(5) (o'clock)

(6) (o'clock)

(7) (o'clock)

(8) (o'clock)

(9) (o'clock)

(10) (o'clock)

(11) (o'clock)

(12) (o'clock)

2 What time is it? Write the time under each clock.

10 points per question

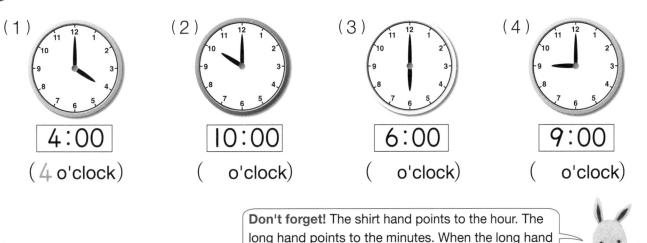

(1) 4:00 (4 o'clock)

(2) 10:00 (o'clock)

(3) 6:00 (o'clock)

(4) 9:00 (o'clock)

Don't forget! The shirt hand points to the hour. The long hand points to the minutes. When the long hand is pointed at 12, it means it's the start of that hour.

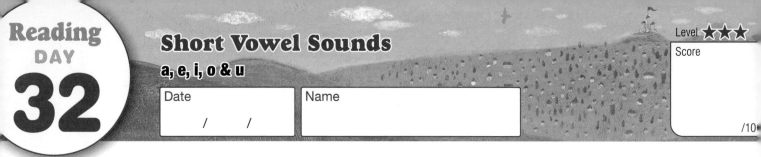

Reading
DAY
32

Short Vowel Sounds
a, e, i, o & u

Date   /   /

Name

Level ★★★

Score

/10

1 Write the correct vowels to finish each rhyming pair of words below.

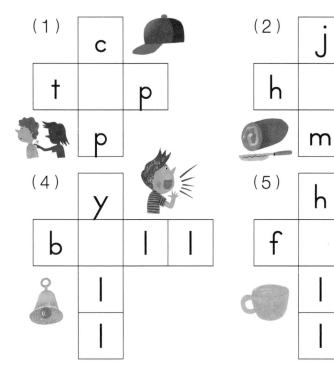

(1)
```
    c
t   p
    p
```

(2)
```
    j
h   m
    m
```

(3)
```
    r
w   d
    d
```

(4)
```
    y
b   l   l
    l
    l
```

(5)
```
    h
f   l   l
    l
    l
```

(6)
```
    c
s   l   d
    l
    d
```

50 points for comple

2 Trace the word below each picture.

50 points for comple

(1) bat

(2) fan

(3) pad

(4) nut

(5) run

(6) mug

(7) ill

(8) nap

(9) dam

(10) six

(11) well

(12) gold

© Kumon Publishing Co.,Ltd.

64

Telling Time

Level ★★★

Score

/100

Math
DAY
33

Date   /   /

Name

1 What time is it? Write the time under each clock.

5 points per question

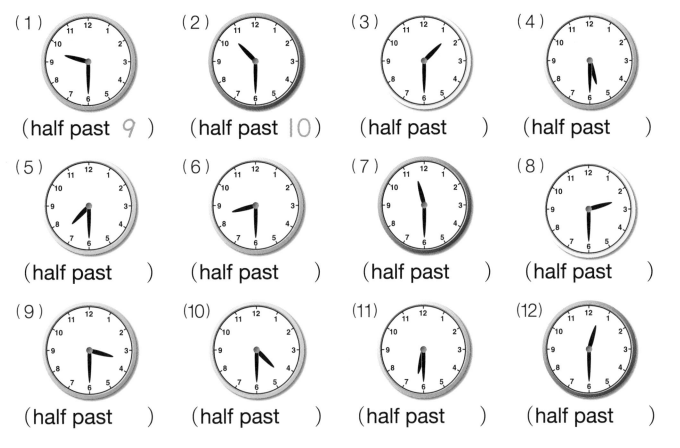

(1) (half past 9)

(2) (half past 10)

(3) (half past   )

(4) (half past   )

(5) (half past   )

(6) (half past   )

(7) (half past   )

(8) (half past   )

(9) (half past   )

(10) (half past   )

(11) (half past   )

(12) (half past   )

2 What time is it? Write the time under each clock.

10 points per question

(1) 5:30 (half past   )

(2) 12:30 (half past   )

(3) 1:30 (half past   )

(4) 8:30 (half past   )

Don't forget! When the long hand is pointed at 6, it is half past that hour.

Reading
DAY
33

Consonant Combinations

Level ★★★
Score

/10

Date   /   /

Name

1 Trace the words below. Then write the words in the blank space. 5 points per question

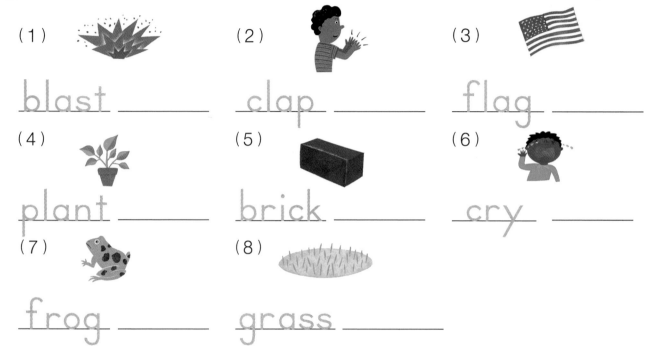

(1)   blast _____

(2)   clap _____

(3)   flag _____

(4)   plant _____

(5)   brick _____

(6)   cry _____

(7)   frog _____

(8)   grass _____

2 Write the beginning of each word and say the word aloud. 10 points per question
Use the pictures as hints.

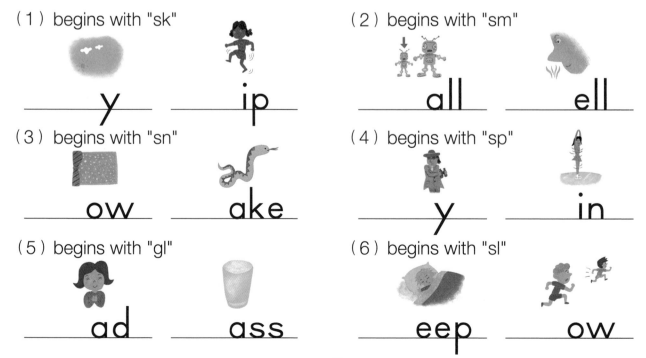

(1) begins with "sk"   ____y   ____ip

(2) begins with "sm"   ____all   ____ell

(3) begins with "sn"   ____ow   ____ake

(4) begins with "sp"   ____y   ____in

(5) begins with "gl"   ____ad   ____ass

(6) begins with "sl"   ____eep   ____ow

Telling Time

Level ★★★

Score

/100

Math
DAY
34

Date   /   /

Name

❶ What time is it? Write the time under each clock.

5 points
per question

(1) (12:00)

(2) (12:30)

(3) (   )

(4) (   )

(5) (   )

(6) (   )

(7) (   )

(8) (   )

(9) (   )

(10) (   )

(11) (   )

(12) (   )

(13) (   )

(14) (   )

(15) (   )

(16) (   )

(17) (   )

(18) (   )

(19) (   )

(20) (   )

© Kumon Publishing Co.,Ltd.

67

Reading
DAY
34

Consonant Combinations

Level ★★★

Score

/100

Date / /

Name

① Trace the words below. Then write the words in the blank space. **5** points per question

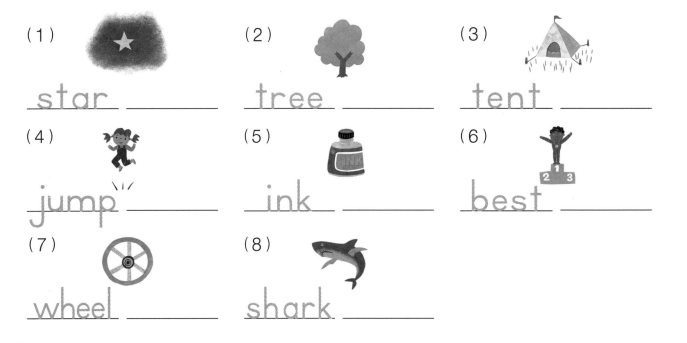

(1) _star_ _____

(2) _tree_ _____

(3) _tent_ _____

(4) _jump_ _____

(5) _ink_ _____

(6) _best_ _____

(7) _wheel_ _____

(8) _shark_ _____

② Write the beginning or ending of each word and say the word aloud. **10** points per question

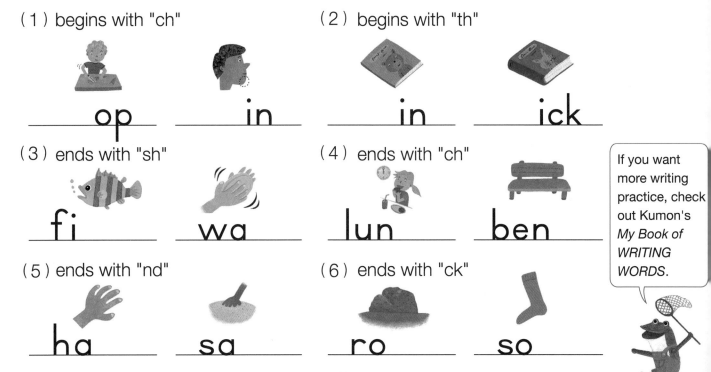

(1) begins with "ch"

_____op   _____in

(2) begins with "th"

_____in   _____ick

(3) ends with "sh"

fi_____   wa_____

(4) ends with "ch"

lun_____   ben_____

(5) ends with "nd"

ha_____   sa_____

(6) ends with "ck"

ro_____   so_____

If you want more writing practice, check out Kumon's *My Book of WRITING WORDS*.

Shapes

Level ★★

Score

/100

Math
DAY
35

Date / /

Name

1 Find the samples shapes below. Then color each shape the 100 points for completion
same color as the sample.

sample ▲ triangle is red.   sample ■ square is blue.

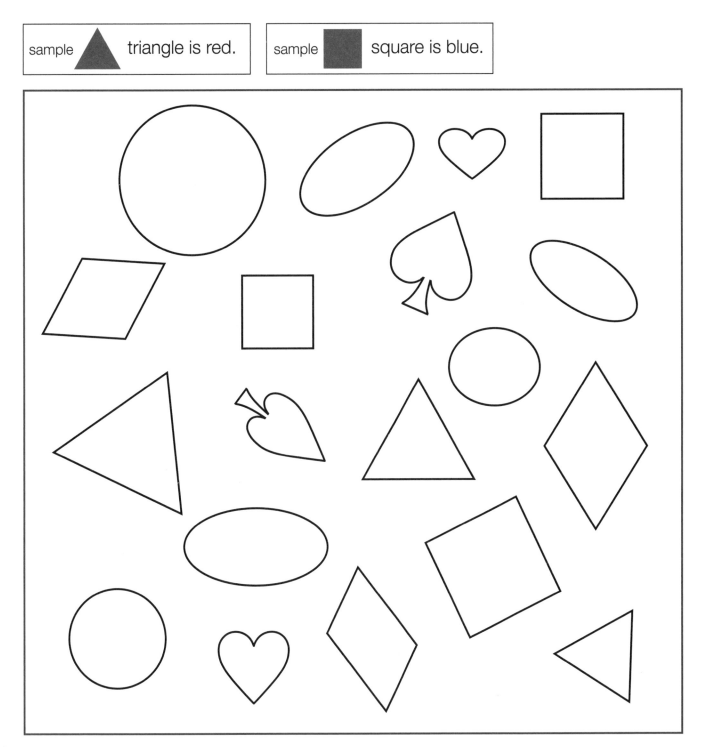

Reading
DAY
35

Long Vowel Sounds
a, e, i, o & u

Level ★★★
Score

/100

Date / /

Name

① Trace the words below and say them aloud. Then connect each word with the correct picture.

10 points per question

(1) mane   •

(2) play   •

(3) hay   •

(4) rain   •

(5) bee   •

(6) feet   •

(7) read   •

(8) fly   •

(9) kite   •

(10) bike   •

• ⓐ
• ⓑ
• ⓒ
• ⓓ
• ⓔ
• ⓕ
• ⓖ
• ⓗ
• ⓘ
• ⓙ

Shapes

Math
DAY
36

1 Find the samples shapes below. Then color each shape the same color as the sample.

100 points for completion

sample ▢ rectangle is green.   sample ● circle is blue.

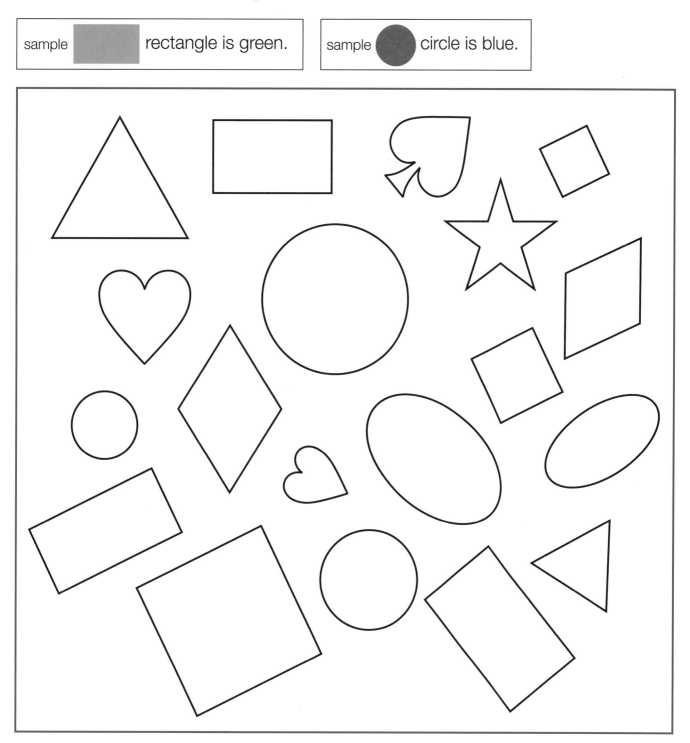

71

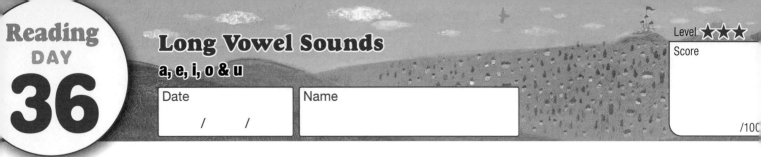

Reading
DAY
36

Long Vowel Sounds
a, e, i, o & u

Date   /   /

Name

Level ★★★

Score

/100

① Trace the words below and say them aloud. Then connect each word with the correct picture.

10 points per question

(1) ride •

(2) cone •

(3) boat •

(4) rose •

(5) toad •

(6) tube •

(7) flute •

(8) dune •

(9) glue •

(10) blue •

• ⓐ

• ⓑ

• ⓒ

• ⓓ

• ⓔ

• ⓕ

• ⓖ

• ⓗ

• ⓘ

• ⓙ

If you want more rhyming practice, check out Kumon's *My Book of RHYMING WORDS LONG VOWELS*.

Counting Coins

Level ★★★

Score

/100

Math
DAY
37

Date   /   /

Name

① Add the value of each row of coins. Then write the amount in the box on the right.   5 points per question

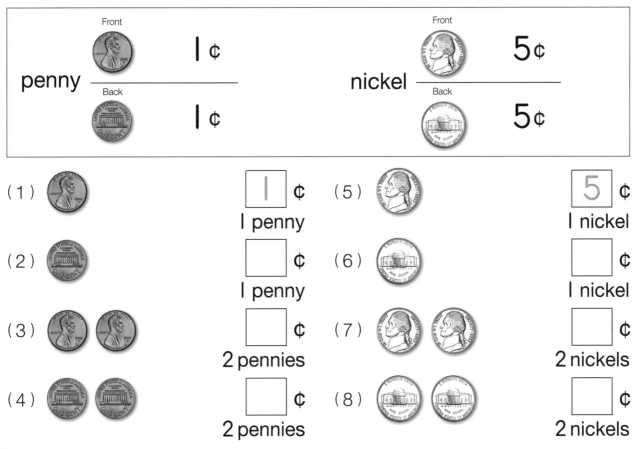

Front
penny
1¢

Back
1¢

Front
nickel
5¢

Back
5¢

(1) ☐ ¢   1 penny

(2) ☐ ¢   1 penny

(3) ☐ ¢   2 pennies

(4) ☐ ¢   2 pennies

(5) 5 ¢   1 nickel

(6) ☐ ¢   1 nickel

(7) ☐ ¢   2 nickels

(8) ☐ ¢   2 nickels

② Add the value of each row of coins. Then write the amount in the box on the right.   10 points per question

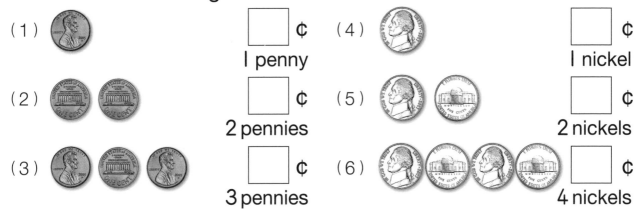

(1) ☐ ¢   1 penny

(2) ☐ ¢   2 pennies

(3) ☐ ¢   3 pennies

(4) ☐ ¢   1 nickel

(5) ☐ ¢   2 nickels

(6) ☐ ¢   4 nickels

Vocabulary
Numbers

Date   /   /

Name

① Count the objects. Then trace the word for the correct number of objects.

5 points per question

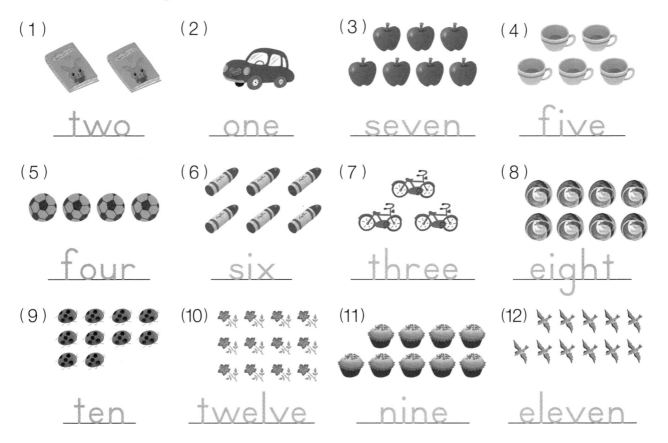

(1)   two

(2)   one

(3)   seven

(4)   five

(5)   four

(6)   six

(7)   three

(8)   eight

(9)   ten

(10)   twelve

(11)   nine

(12)   eleven

② Color the picture according to each sentence below.

40 points for comple

(1) Color five flowers.

(2) Color three birds.

(3) Color two bathing suits.

(4) Color four shirts.

Counting Coins

Date   /   /

Name

1 Add the value of each row of coins. Then write the amount in the box on the right.

5 points per question

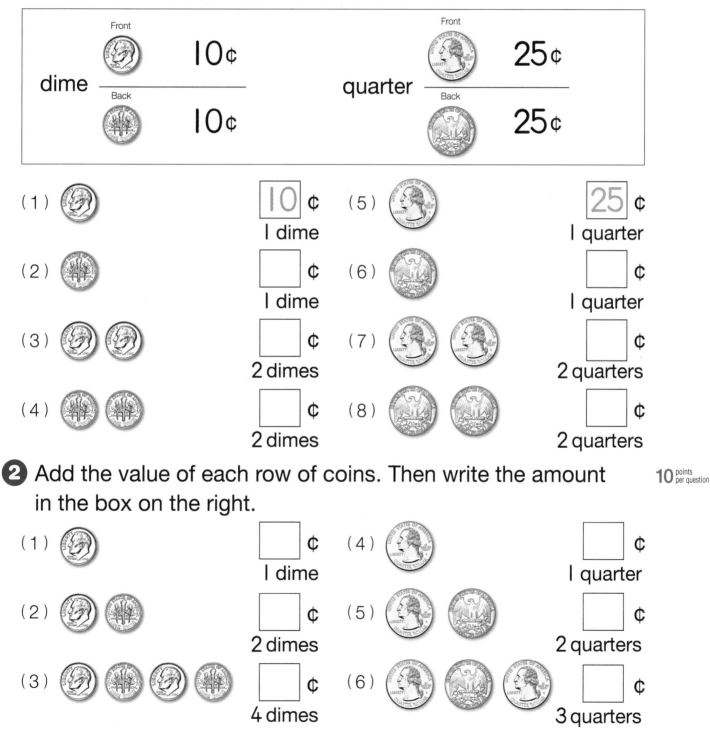

dime Front	10¢	
Back	10¢	
quarter Front	25¢	
Back	25¢	

(1) ☐ 10 ¢
I dime

(2) ☐ ¢
I dime

(3) ☐ ¢
2 dimes

(4) ☐ ¢
2 dimes

(5) ☐ 25 ¢
I quarter

(6) ☐ ¢
I quarter

(7) ☐ ¢
2 quarters

(8) ☐ ¢
2 quarters

2 Add the value of each row of coins. Then write the amount in the box on the right.

10 points per question

(1) ☐ ¢
I dime

(2) ☐ ¢
2 dimes

(3) ☐ ¢
4 dimes

(4) ☐ ¢
I quarter

(5) ☐ ¢
2 quarters

(6) ☐ ¢
3 quarters

Vocabulary
Colors

Date   /   /

Name

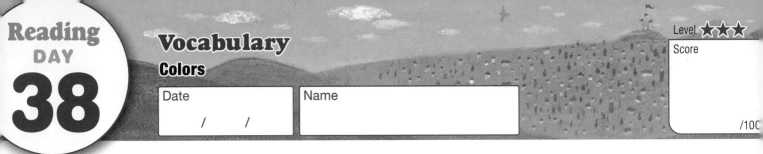

① Look at the picture. Then trace the words shown and read the phrase aloud.

5 points per question

(1)
red
ball

(2)
orange
fish

(3)
yellow
kite

(4)
green
yo-yo

(5)
blue
water

(6)
purple
shoe

(7)
brown
cow

(8)
white
goat

② Color the picture according to each sentence below.

60 points for completi

(1) Color the plums purple.

(2) Color the apples red.

(3) Color the cheese orange.

(4) Color the broccoli green.

(5) Color the blueberries blue.

(6) Color the lemons yellow.

(7) Color the bread brown.

(8) Color the cake white.

Counting Coins

Level ★★★

Score

/100

Math
DAY
39

Date / /

Name

1 Add the value of each group of coins. Then write the amount in the box on the right.

5 points per question

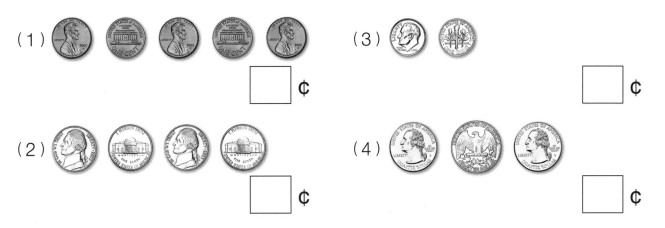

(1) ☐ ¢

(2) ☐ ¢

(3) ☐ ¢

(4) ☐ ¢

2 Add the value of each group of coins. Then write the amount in the box on the right.

10 points per question

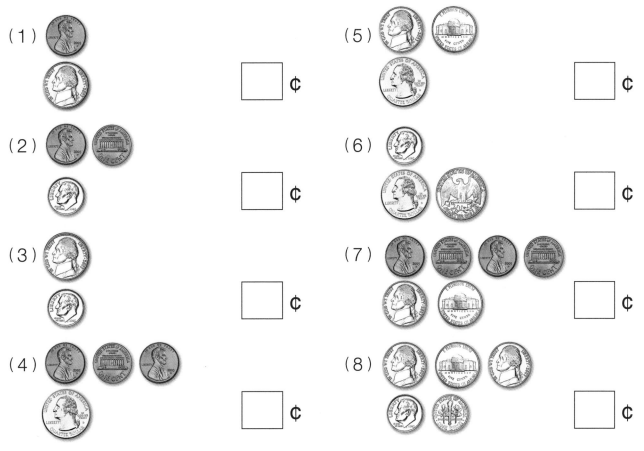

(1) ☐ ¢

(2) ☐ ¢

(3) ☐ ¢

(4) ☐ ¢

(5) ☐ ¢

(6) ☐ ¢

(7) ☐ ¢

(8) ☐ ¢

Reading DAY 39

Vocabulary
Shapes

Date / /

Name

Level ★★★
Score

/10

1 Trace the words shown on the train below.

10 points per question

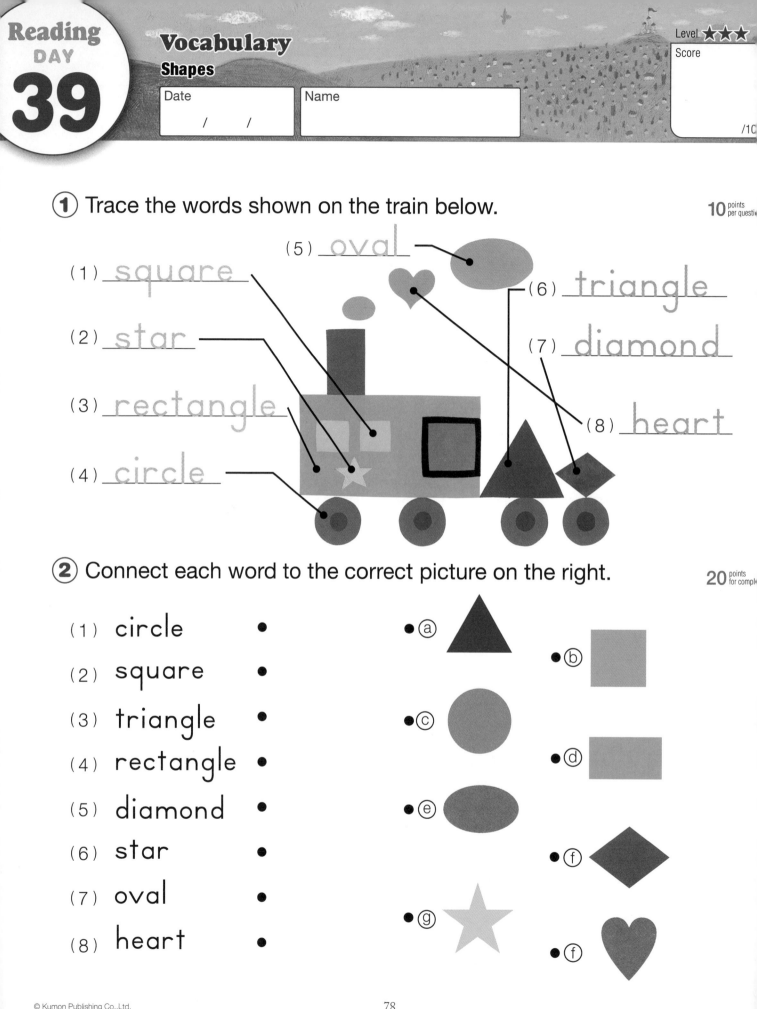

(1) square

(2) star

(3) rectangle

(4) circle

(5) oval

(6) triangle

(7) diamond

(8) heart

2 Connect each word to the correct picture on the right.

20 points for complete

(1) circle •

(2) square •

(3) triangle •

(4) rectangle •

(5) diamond •

(6) star •

(7) oval •

(8) heart •

• ⓐ

• ⓑ

• ⓒ

• ⓓ

• ⓔ

• ⓕ

• ⓖ

• ⓕ

Weight

Level ★★★

Score

/100

Math
DAY

40

Date

/ /

Name

① Which object is heavier? Circle the heavier object.

10 points per question

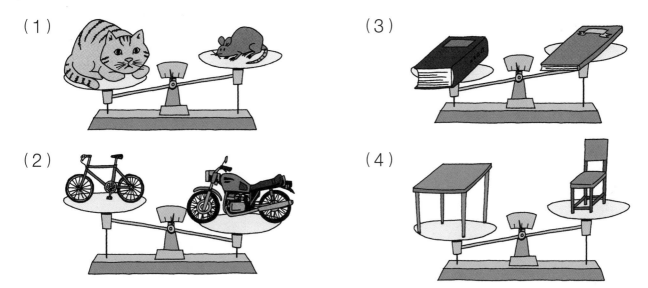

(1)

(2)

(3)

(4)

② Each block is the same size and weight. Circle the heavier group of blocks.

10 points per question

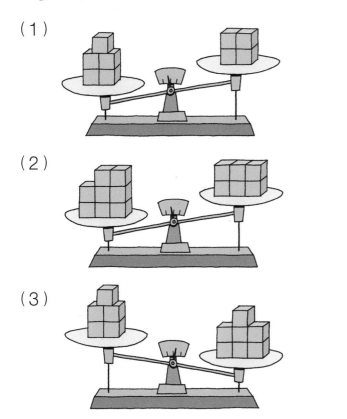

(1)

(2)

(3)

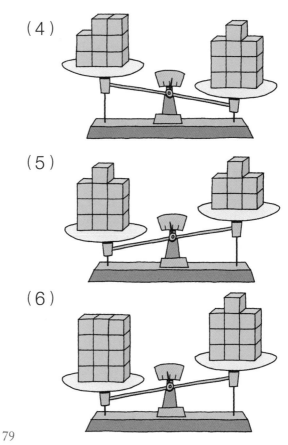

(4)

(5)

(6)

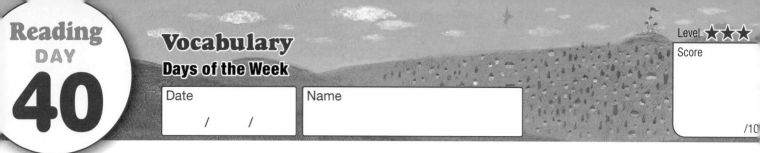

Vocabulary
Days of the Week

Date   /   /

Name

① Look at the calendar. Then trace the correct word in each sentence and read the sentence aloud.

100 points for com

(1) On __Monday__, I start school.

(2) On __Tuesday__, I play soccer.

(3) On __Wednesday__, I read a book.

(4) On __Thursday__, I practice the violin.

(5) On __Friday__, I watch a movie.

(6) On __Saturday__, I go to the park.

(7) On __Sunday__, I help cook.

Monday	Tuesday	Wednesday	Thursday	Friday	Saturday	Sunday

Let's learn every day of the week!

Length

Date
/   /

Name

1 Compare the length of the two pencils shown in ⓐ and ⓑ, and circle the longer one.

10 points per question

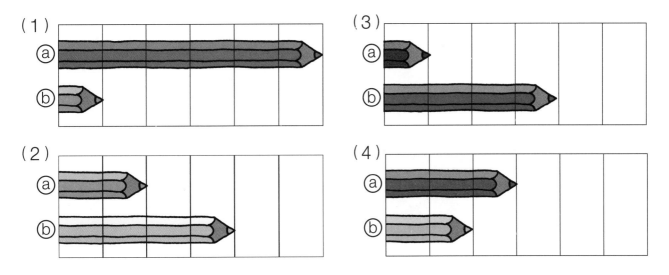

(1)
ⓐ
ⓑ

(3)
ⓐ
ⓑ

(2)
ⓐ
ⓑ

(4)
ⓐ
ⓑ

2 Compare the length of the two lines shown in ⓐ and ⓑ, and write a ✓ longer one.

15 points per question

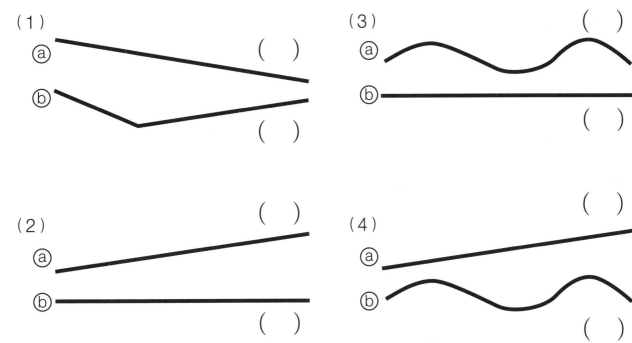

(1)
ⓐ   (   )
ⓑ
           (   )

(3)   (   )
ⓐ
ⓑ
           (   )

(2)   (   )
ⓐ
ⓑ
           (   )

(4)   (   )
ⓐ
ⓑ
           (   )

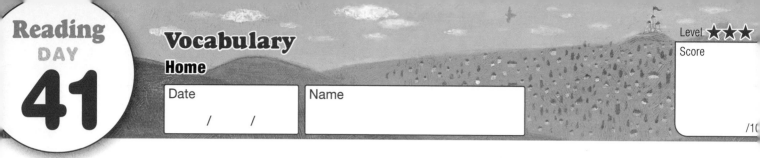

Vocabulary

Home

Date	Name
/ /	

Level ★★★

Score

/10

① Trace the words shown in the kitchen below.

5 points per question

(1) sink

(2) bowl

(3) fork

(4) chair

(5) pot

(6) table

(7) mug

(8) napkin

② Connect each word to the correct object on the right.

60 points for comp

(1) door •

(2) roof •

(3) car •

(4) mailbox •

(5) tree •

(6) house •

(7) flag •

(8) bicycle •

Area

Level ★★★

Score

/100

Math
DAY
42

Date / /

Name

1 Which is larger? Circle the larger object.

10 points per question

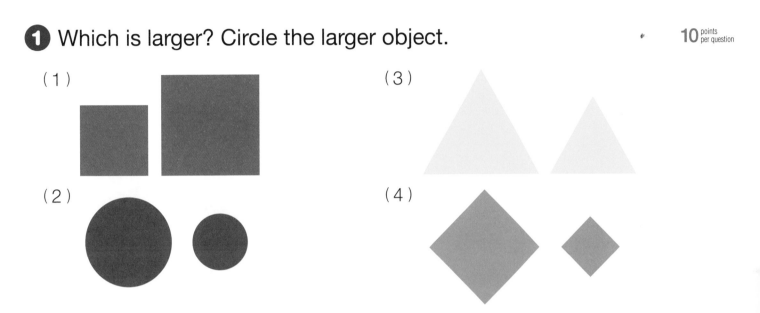

(1)

(2)

(3)

(4)

2 Below are some objects covered by squares of colored paper. Which is larger? Write a ✓ below to the larger one.

10 points per question

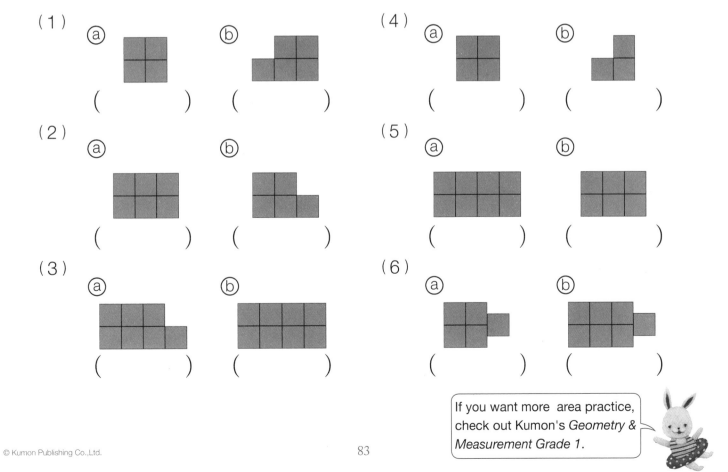

(1)   ⓐ   ( )   ⓑ   ( )

(2)   ⓐ   ( )   ⓑ   ( )

(3)   ⓐ   ( )   ⓑ   ( )

(4)   ⓐ   ( )   ⓑ   ( )

(5)   ⓐ   ( )   ⓑ   ( )

(6)   ⓐ   ( )   ⓑ   ( )

If you want more area practice, check out Kumon's *Geometry & Measurement Grade 1.*

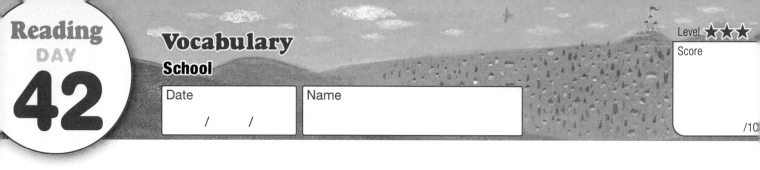

Vocabulary
School

Level ★★★

Date / /

Name

Score

/10

① Trace the words shown in the classroom below.

5 points per question

(1) clock

(2) book

(3) desk

(4) chair

(5) chalk

(6) pencil

(7) paint

(8) cut

② Write the name of each object or action. Use the pictures as hints. 60 point for comp

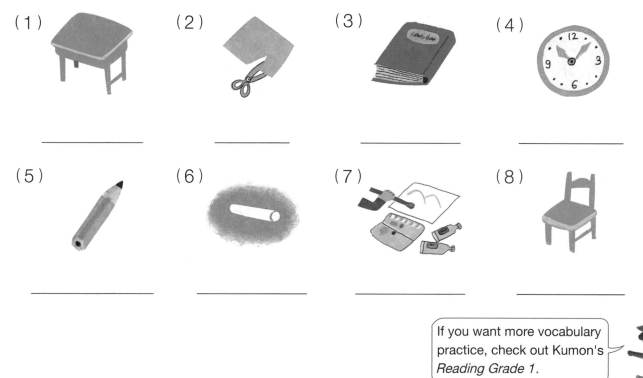

(1)

(2)

(3)

(4)

_____

_____

_____

_____

(5)

(6)

(7)

(8)

_____

_____

_____

_____

If you want more vocabulary practice, check out Kumon's *Reading Grade 1*.

Review

Level ★★★
Score

Math
DAY
43

Date
    /   /

Name

/100

1 Fill in the missing numbers.

40 points for completion

1	2	3	4		6		8		
11			15		17		19		
	22		24	25	26		28		30
31		33		35		37	38	39	
	42	43	44		46			49	50

2 Add.

6 points per question

(1) $5 + 2 =$

(2) $8 + 1 =$

(3) $1 + 1 =$

(4) $2 + 2 =$

(5) $3 + 2 =$

(6) $4 + 2 =$

(7) $6 + 1 =$

(8) $10 + 1 =$

(9) $7 + 2 =$

(10) $9 + 2 =$

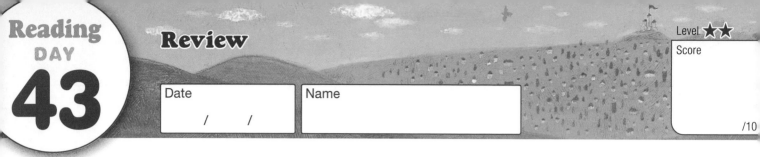

① Write the uppercase letters in the table below.

100 points for comp

A	B	C	D	E	F

G	H	I	J	K	L

M	N	O	P	Q	R

S	T	U	V	W	X

Y	Z

You're almost at the end and you've made great progress!

Review

Level ★★★
Score

/100

Math
DAY
44

Date
/   /

Name

1 Fill in the missing numbers.

40 points for completion

51	52	53		55		57		59	
	62	63	64		66		68	69	70
71		73	74	75		77		79	
	82	83	84		86		88		90
91	92			95	96	97			

2 Subtract.

6 points per question

(1) 5 − 2 =

(2) 8 − 1 =

(3) 7 − 2 =

(4) 4 − 2 =

(5) 6 − 1 =

(6) 9 − 2 =

(7) 3 − 1 =

(8) 8 − 2 =

(9) 10 − 2 =

(10) 2 − 1 =

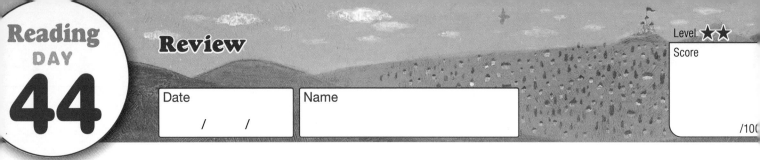

Reading
DAY
44

Review

Date   /   /

Name

Level ★★

Score

/100

1 Write the lowercase letters in the table below.

100 points for comple

a	b	c	d	e	f

g	h	i	j	k	l

m	n	o	p	q	r

s	t	u	v	w	x

y	z

Super job! When you're done, take a bow.

Review

Level ★★★

Score

/100

Math
DAY
45

Date
/   /

Name

1 What time is it? Write the time under each clock.   10 points per question

(1)   (2)   (3)   (4)

(   )   (   )   (   )   (   )

2 Add the value of each group of coins. Then write the amount   10 points per question
in the box on the right.

(1)   ☐ ¢   (3)   ☐ ¢

(2)   ☐ ¢   (4)   ☐ ¢

3 Color the below shape in red.   20 points for completion

sample ▦ square is red.

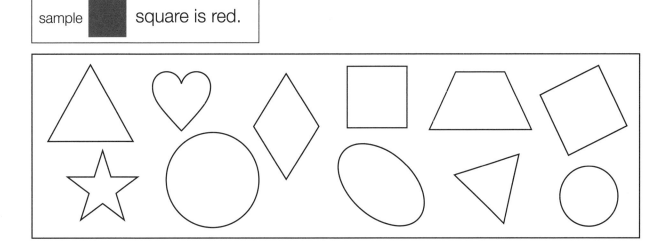

Review

Date   /   /

Name

① Write the correct vowels to finish each word below. Use the pictures as hints.

4 points per question

(1) c__t

(2) p__n

(3) p__g

(4) f__x

(5) c__b

② Write the beginning of each word below and say the word aloud. Use the pictures as hints.

5 points per question

(1) ___y

(2) ___ag

(3) ___ee

(4) ___ant

③ Pick the correct word from the box to match each picture and write it below.

6 points per question

red mane cone desk circle bee rose kite flute mug

(1) _____

(2) _____

(3) _____

(4) _____

(5) _____

(6) _____

(7) _____

(8) _____

(9) _____

(10) _____

DAY 1, pages 1 & 2

DAY 2, pages 3 & 4

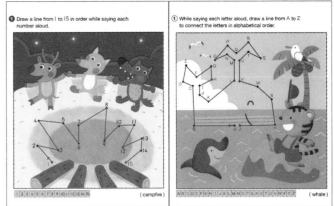

DAY 3, pages 5 & 6

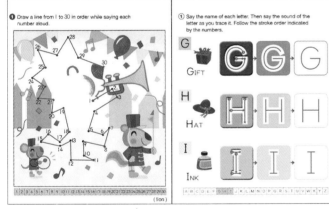

DAY 4, pages 7 & 8

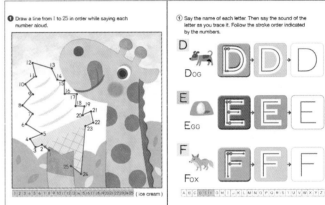

DAY 5, pages 9 & 10

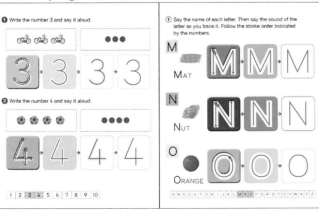

DAY 6, pages 11 & 12

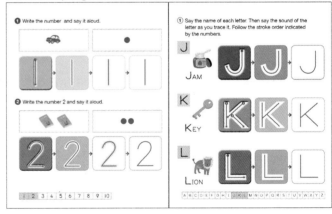

DAY 7, pages 13 & 14

DAY 8, pages 15 & 16

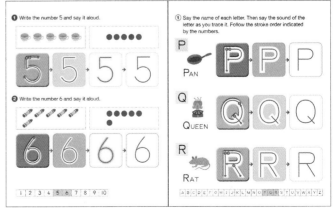

DAY 9, pages 17 & 18

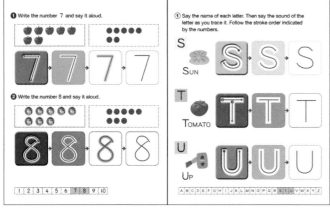

DAY 10, pages 19 & 20

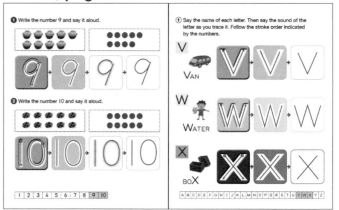

DAY 11, pages 21 & 22

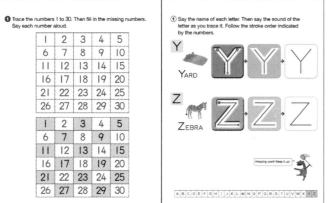

DAY 12, pages 23 & 24

DAY 13, pages 25 & 26

DAY 14, pages 27 & 28

DAY 15, pages 29 & 30

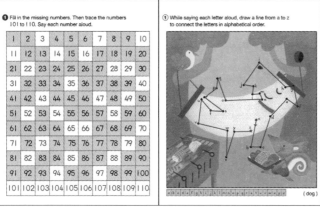

(dog)

DAY 16, pages 31 & 32

(sea lion)

DAY 17, pages 33 & 34

❶ Fill in the missing numbers. Say each number aloud.

1	2	3	4	5	6	7	8	9	10
11	12	13	14	15	16	17	18	19	20
21	22	23	24	25	26	27	28	29	30
31	32	33	34	35	36	37	38	39	40
41	42	43	44	45	46	47	48	49	50
51	52	53	54	55	56	57	58	59	60
61	62	63	64	65	66	67	68	69	70
71	72	73	74	75	76	77	78	79	80
81	82	83	84	85	86	87	88	89	90
91	92	93	94	95	96	97	98	99	100
101	102	103	104	105	106	107	108	109	110
111	112	113	114	115	116	117	118	119	120

① Say the name of each letter. Then say the sound of the letter as you trace it. Follow the stroke order indicated by the numbers.

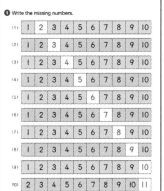

apple a → a → a
bed b → b → b
Cup c → c → c

DAY 18, pages 35 & 36

❶ Write the missing numbers.

(1) 1 2 3 4 5 6 7 8 9 10
(2) 1 2 3 4 5 6 7 8 9 10
(3) 1 2 3 4 5 6 7 8 9 10
(4) 1 2 3 4 5 6 7 8 9 10
(5) 1 2 3 4 5 6 7 8 9 10
(6) 1 2 3 4 5 6 7 8 9 10
(7) 1 2 3 4 5 6 7 8 9 10
(8) 1 2 3 4 5 6 7 8 9 10
(9) 1 2 3 4 5 6 7 8 9 10
(10) 2 3 4 5 6 7 8 9 10 11

① Say the name of each letter. Then say the sound of the letter as you trace it. Follow the stroke order indicated by the numbers.

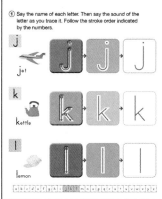

duck d → d → d
elephant e → e → e
frog f → f → f

DAY 19, pages 37 & 38

❶ Read each number sentence aloud. Trace the answer in the number line. Then write the answer in the number sentence.

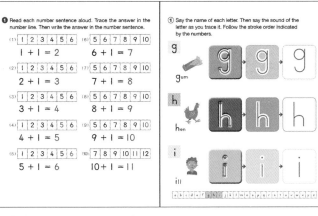

(1) 1 2 3 4 5 6   1 + 1 = 2
(2) 1 2 3 4 5 6   2 + 1 = 3
(3) 1 2 3 4 5 6   3 + 1 = 4
(4) 1 2 3 4 5 6   4 + 1 = 5
(5) 1 2 3 4 5 6   5 + 1 = 6
(6) 5 6 7 8 9 10   6 + 1 = 7
(7) 5 6 7 8 9 10   7 + 1 = 8
(8) 5 6 7 8 9 10   8 + 1 = 9
(9) 5 6 7 8 9 10   9 + 1 = 10
(10) 7 8 9 10 11 12   10 + 1 = 11

① Say the name of each letter. Then say the sound of the letter as you trace it. Follow the stroke order indicated by the numbers.

gum g → g → g
hen h → h → h
ill i → i → i

DAY 20, pages 39 & 40

❶ Add the numbers. Use the number line as a guide.

1 2 3 4 5 6 7 8 9 10 11 12 13 14 15

(1) 1 + 1 = 2
(2) 2 + 1 = 3
(3) 3 + 1 = 4
(4) 4 + 1 = 5
(5) 5 + 1 = 6
(6) 6 + 1 = 7
(7) 7 + 1 = 8
(8) 8 + 1 = 9
(9) 9 + 1 = 10
(10) 10 + 1 = 11

❷ Add.

(1) 4 + 1 = 5
(2) 5 + 1 = 6
(3) 1 + 1 = 2
(4) 2 + 1 = 3
(5) 8 + 1 = 9
(6) 3 + 1 = 4
(7) 6 + 1 = 7
(8) 7 + 1 = 8
(9) 9 + 1 = 10
(10) 10 + 1 = 11

① Say the name of each letter. Then say the sound of the letter as you trace it. Follow the stroke order indicated by the numbers.

jet j → j → j
kettle k → k → k
lemon l → l → l

DAY 21, pages 41 & 42

❶ Write the missing numbers.

(1) 1 2 3 4 5 6 7 8 9 10
(2) 1 2 3 4 5 6 7 8 9 10
(3) 1 2 3 4 5 6 7 8 9 10
(4) 1 2 3 4 5 6 7 8 9 10
(5) 1 2 3 4 5 6 7 8 9 10
(6) 1 2 3 4 5 6 7 8 9 10
(7) 1 2 3 4 5 6 7 8 9 10
(8) 1 2 3 4 5 6 7 8 9 10
(9) 2 3 4 5 6 7 8 9 10 11
(10) 3 4 5 6 7 8 9 10 11 12

① Say the name of each letter. Then say the sound of the letter as you trace it. Follow the stroke order indicated by the numbers.

milk m → m → m
net n → n → n
Octopus o → o → o

DAY 22, pages 43 & 44

❶ Read each number sentence aloud. Trace the answer in the number line. Then write the answer in the number sentence.

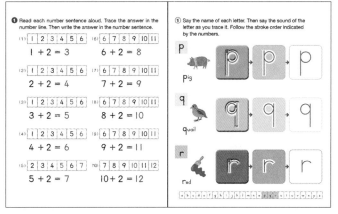

(1) 1 2 3 4 5 6   1 + 2 = 3
(2) 1 2 3 4 5 6   2 + 2 = 4
(3) 1 2 3 4 5 6   3 + 2 = 5
(4) 1 2 3 4 5 6   4 + 2 = 6
(5) 2 3 4 5 6 7   5 + 2 = 7
(6) 6 7 8 9 10 11   6 + 2 = 8
(7) 6 7 8 9 10 11   7 + 2 = 9
(8) 6 7 8 9 10 11   8 + 2 = 10
(9) 6 7 8 9 10 11   9 + 2 = 11
(10) 7 8 9 10 11 12   10 + 2 = 12

① Say the name of each letter. Then say the sound of the letter as you trace it. Follow the stroke order indicated by the numbers.

pig p → p → p
quail q → q → q
red r → r → r

DAY 23, pages 45 & 46

❶ Add the numbers. Use the number line as a guide.

1 2 3 4 5 6 7 8 9 10 11 12 13 14 15

(1) 1 + 2 = 3
(2) 2 + 2 = 4
(3) 3 + 2 = 5
(4) 4 + 2 = 6
(5) 5 + 2 = 7
(6) 6 + 2 = 8
(7) 7 + 2 = 9
(8) 8 + 2 = 10
(9) 9 + 2 = 11
(10) 10 + 2 = 12

❷ Add.

(1) 1 + 2 = 3
(2) 5 + 2 = 7
(3) 6 + 2 = 8
(4) 3 + 2 = 5
(5) 4 + 2 = 6
(6) 7 + 2 = 9
(7) 8 + 2 = 10
(8) 2 + 2 = 4
(9) 9 + 2 = 11
(10) 10 + 2 = 12

① Say the name of each letter. Then say the sound of the letter as you trace it. Follow the stroke order indicated by the numbers.

Sand s → s → s
tent t → t → t
Umbrella u → u → u

DAY 24, pages 47 & 48

❶ Add the numbers.

(1) 3 + 1 = 4
(2) 5 + 2 = 7
(3) 8 + 1 = 9
(4) 6 + 1 = 7
(5) 4 + 2 = 6
(6) 7 + 1 = 8
(7) 5 + 1 = 6
(8) 8 + 2 = 10
(9) 1 + 2 = 3
(10) 9 + 1 = 10
(11) 6 + 2 = 8
(12) 10 + 1 = 11
(13) 2 + 1 = 3
(14) 3 + 2 = 5
(15) 2 + 2 = 4
(16) 4 + 1 = 5
(17) 1 + 1 = 2
(18) 7 + 2 = 9
(19) 9 + 2 = 11
(20) 10 + 2 = 12

① Say the name of each letter. Then say the sound of the letter as you trace it. Follow the stroke order indicated by the numbers.

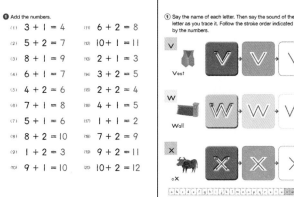
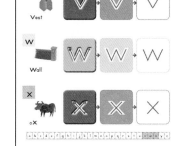

Vest v → v → v
Wall w → w → w
oX x → x → x

DAY 25, pages 49 & 50

❶ Write the missing numbers.

(1) 10 9 8 7 6 5 4 3 2 1
(2) 10 9 8 7 6 5 4 3 2 1
(3) 10 9 8 7 6 5 4 3 2 1
(4) 10 9 8 7 6 5 4 3 2 1
(5) 10 9 8 7 6 5 4 3 2 1
(6) 10 9 8 7 6 5 4 3 2 1
(7) 10 9 8 7 6 5 4 3 2 1
(8) 10 9 8 7 6 5 4 3 2 1
(9) 10 9 8 7 6 5 4 3 2 1
(10) 11 10 9 8 7 6 5 4 3 2

❶ Say the name of each letter. Then say the sound of the letter as you trace it. Follow the stroke order indicated by the numbers.

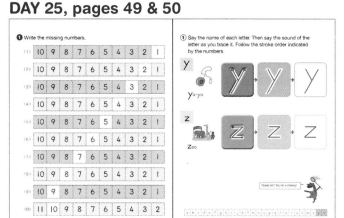

y-yo

z-oo

DAY 26, pages 51 & 52

❶ Read each number sentence aloud. Trace the answer in the number line. Then write the answer in the number sentence.

(1) 6 5 4 3 2 1
2 − 1 = 1

(6) 10 9 8 7 6 5
7 − 1 = 6

(2) 6 5 4 3 2 1
3 − 1 = 2

(7) 10 9 8 7 6 5
8 − 1 = 7

(3) 6 5 4 3 2 1
4 − 1 = 3

(8) 10 9 8 7 6 5
9 − 1 = 8

(4) 6 5 4 3 2 1
5 − 1 = 4

(9) 10 9 8 7 6 5
10 − 1 = 9

(5) 6 5 4 3 2 1
6 − 1 = 5

(10) 11 10 9 8 7 6
11 − 1 = 10

❶ Trace the letters "a" to "z" while saying each letter aloud.

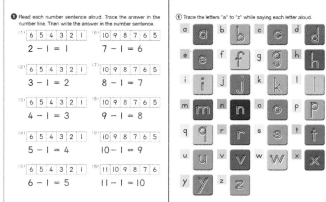

DAY 27, pages 53 & 54

❶ Subtract the numbers. Use the number line as a guide.

15 14 13 12 11 10 9 8 7 6 5 4 3 2 1

(1) 2 − 1 = 1
(6) 7 − 1 = 6
(2) 3 − 1 = 2
(7) 8 − 1 = 7
(3) 4 − 1 = 3
(8) 9 − 1 = 8
(4) 5 − 1 = 4
(9) 10 − 1 = 9
(5) 6 − 1 = 5
(10) 11 − 1 = 10

❷ Subtract.

(1) 5 − 1 = 4
(6) 8 − 1 = 7
(2) 3 − 1 = 2
(7) 4 − 1 = 3
(3) 6 − 1 = 5
(8) 10 − 1 = 9
(4) 7 − 1 = 6
(9) 2 − 1 = 1
(5) 9 − 1 = 8
(10) 11 − 1 = 10

❶ Trace the letters "a" to "z" while saying each letter aloud.

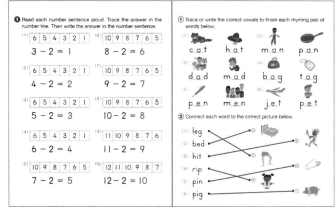

DAY 28, pages 55 & 56

❶ Trace the numbers in each number line. Then write the missing numbers.

(1) 10 9 8 7 6 5 4 3 2 1
(2) 10 9 8 7 6 5 4 3 2 1
(3) 10 9 8 7 6 5 4 3 2 1
(4) 10 9 8 7 6 5 4 3 2 1
(5) 10 9 8 7 6 5 4 3 2 1
(6) 10 9 8 7 6 5 4 3 2 1
(7) 10 9 8 7 6 5 4 3 2 1
(8) 10 9 8 7 6 5 4 3 2 1
(9) 11 10 9 8 7 6 5 4 3 2
(10) 12 11 10 9 8 7 6 5 4 3

❶ Trace the letters "a" to "z" while saying each letter aloud.

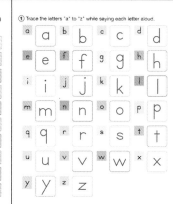

DAY 29, pages 57 & 58

❶ Read each number sentence aloud. Trace the answer in the number line. Then write the answer in the number sentence.

(1) 6 5 4 3 2 1
3 − 2 = 1

(6) 10 9 8 7 6 5
8 − 2 = 6

(2) 6 5 4 3 2 1
4 − 2 = 2

(7) 10 9 8 7 6 5
9 − 2 = 7

(3) 6 5 4 3 2 1
5 − 2 = 3

(8) 10 9 8 7 6 5
10 − 2 = 8

(4) 6 5 4 3 2 1
6 − 2 = 4

(9) 11 10 9 8 7 6
11 − 2 = 9

(5) 10 9 8 7 6 5
7 − 2 = 5

(10) 12 11 10 9 8 7
12 − 2 = 10

❶ Trace or write the correct vowels to finish each rhyming pair of words below.

(1) c a t (2) h a t (3) m a n (4) p a n
(3) d a d (4) m a d (5) b a g (6) t a g
(5) p e n (6) m e n (7) j e t (8) p e t

❷ Connect each word to the correct picture below.

(1) leg
(2) bed
(3) hit
(4) rip
(5) pin
(6) pig

DAY 30, pages 59 & 60

❶ Subtract the numbers. Use the number line as a guide.

15 14 13 12 11 10 9 8 7 6 5 4 3 2 1

(1) 3 − 2 = 1
(6) 8 − 2 = 6
(2) 4 − 2 = 2
(7) 9 − 2 = 7
(3) 5 − 2 = 3
(8) 10 − 2 = 8
(4) 6 − 2 = 4
(9) 11 − 2 = 9
(5) 7 − 2 = 5
(10) 12 − 2 = 10

❷ Subtract.

(1) 5 − 2 = 3
(6) 8 − 2 = 6
(2) 3 − 2 = 1
(7) 4 − 2 = 2
(3) 6 − 2 = 4
(8) 10 − 2 = 8
(4) 7 − 2 = 5
(9) 12 − 2 = 10
(5) 9 − 2 = 7
(10) 11 − 2 = 9

❶ Trace or write the correct vowels to finish each rhyming pair of words below.

(1) k i d (2) l i d (3) l o g (4) h o g
(3) d o t (4) h o t (5) f o x (6) b o x
(5) r o b (6) j o b (7) h o p (8) m o p

❷ Connect each word to the correct picture below.

(1) hug
(2) hum
(3) cub
(4) sun
(5) cut
(6) pup

DAY 31, pages 61 & 62

❶ Subtract.

(1) 3 − 1 = 2
(11) 6 − 2 = 4
(2) 5 − 2 = 3
(12) 10 − 1 = 9
(3) 8 − 1 = 7
(13) 2 − 1 = 1
(4) 6 − 1 = 5
(14) 3 − 2 = 1
(5) 4 − 2 = 2
(15) 12 − 2 = 10
(6) 7 − 1 = 6
(16) 4 − 1 = 3
(7) 5 − 1 = 4
(17) 11 − 1 = 10
(8) 8 − 2 = 6
(18) 7 − 2 = 5
(9) 11 − 2 = 9
(19) 9 − 2 = 7
(10) 9 − 1 = 8
(20) 10 − 2 = 8

❶ Write the correct vowels to finish each rhyming pair of words below.

(1) b e g (2) m i x (3) p i t
(4) d i p (5) b i n (6) w i g

❷ Trace the word below each picture.

(1) ox (2) sob (3) top (4) rag
(5) hen (6) wet (7) hid (8) fog
(9) pot (10) bug (11) gum (12) tub

DAY 32, pages 63 & 64

❶ What time is it? Write the time under each clock.

(1) 1 o'clock (2) 2 o'clock (3) 3 o'clock (4) 5 o'clock
(5) 6 o'clock (6) 4 o'clock (7) 7 o'clock (8) 9 o'clock
(9) 10 o'clock (10) 11 o'clock (11) 8 o'clock (12) 12 o'clock

❷ What time is it? Write the time under each clock.

(1) 4:00 (2) 10:00 (3) 6:00 (4) 9:00
(1 o'clock) (10 o'clock) (6 o'clock) (9 o'clock)

❶ Write the correct vowels to finish each rhyming pair of words below.

(1) t a p (2) h a m (3) w e d
(4) p ___ (5) m ___ (6) d ___
(7) b e l l (8) f i l l (9) s o l d

❷ Trace the word below each picture.

(1) bat (2) fan (3) pad (4) nut
(5) run (6) mug (7) ill (8) nap
(9) dam (10) six (11) well (12) gold

DAY 33, pages 65 & 66

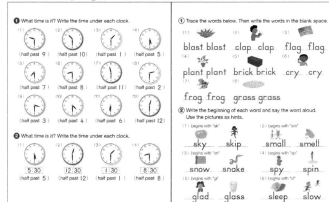

DAY 34, pages 67 & 68

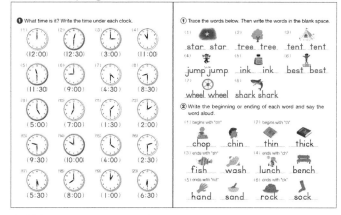

DAY 35, pages 69 & 70

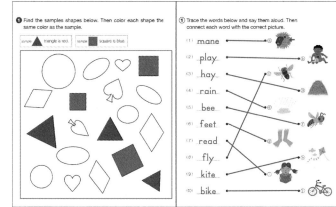

DAY 36, pages 71 & 72

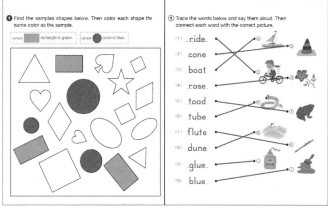

DAY 37, pages 73 & 74

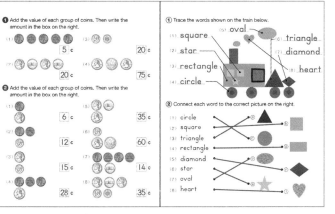

DAY 38, pages 75 & 76

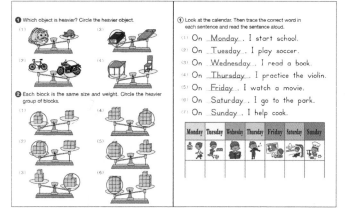

DAY 39, pages 77 & 78

DAY 40, pages 79 & 80

DAY 41, pages 81 & 82

❶ Compare the length of the two pencils shown in ⓐ and ⓑ, and circle the longer one.

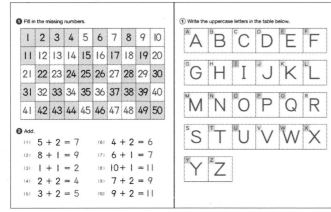

(1) (3)
(2) (4)

❷ Compare the length of the two lines shown in ⓐ and ⓑ, and write a ✓ longer one.

(1) (✓)
(2) (✓)
(3) (✓)
(4) (✓)

① Trace the words shown in the kitchen below.

(1) sink
(2) bowl
(3) fork
(4) chair
(5) pot
(6) table
(7) mug
(8) napkin

② Connect each word to the correct object on the right.

(1) door
(2) roof
(3) car
(4) mailbox
(5) tree
(6) house
(7) flag
(8) bicycle

DAY 42, pages 83 & 84

❶ Which is larger? Circle the larger object.

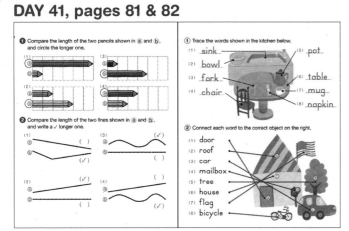

(1) (2) (3) (4)

❷ Below are some objects covered by squares of colored paper. Which is larger? Write a ✓ below to the larger one.

(1) ⓐ ( ) ⓑ (✓)   (4) ( ) (✓)
(2) ( ) (✓)   (5) (✓) ( )
(3) (✓) ( )   (6) ( ) (✓)

① Trace the words shown in the classroom below.

(1) clock
(2) book
(3) desk
(4) chair
(5) chalk
(6) pencil
(7) paint
(8) cut

② Write the name of each object or action. Use the pictures as hints.

(1) desk
(2) cut
(3) book
(4) clock
(5) pencil
(6) chalk
(7) paint
(8) chair

DAY 43, pages 85 & 86

❶ Fill in the missing numbers.

1	2	3	4	5	6	7	8	9	10
11	12	13	14	15	16	17	18	19	20
21	22	23	24	25	26	27	28	29	30
31	32	33	34	35	36	37	38	39	40
41	42	43	44	45	46	47	48	49	50

❷ Add.

(1) 5 + 2 = 7
(2) 8 + 1 = 9
(3) 1 + 1 = 2
(4) 2 + 2 = 4
(5) 3 + 2 = 5
(6) 4 + 2 = 6
(7) 6 + 1 = 7
(8) 10 + 1 = 11
(9) 7 + 2 = 9
(10) 9 + 2 = 11

① Write the uppercase letters in the table below.

A	B	C	D	E	F
G	H	I	J	K	L
M	N	O	P	Q	R
S	T	U	V	W	X
Y	Z				

DAY 44, pages 87 & 88

❶ Fill in the missing numbers.

51	52	53	54	55	56	57	58	59	60
61	62	63	64	65	66	67	68	69	70
71	72	73	74	75	76	77	78	79	80
81	82	83	84	85	86	87	88	89	90
91	92	93	94	95	96	97	98	99	100

❷ Subtract.

(1) 5 - 2 = 3
(2) 8 - 1 = 7
(3) 7 - 2 = 5
(4) 4 - 2 = 2
(5) 6 - 1 = 5
(6) 9 - 2 = 7
(7) 3 - 1 = 2
(8) 8 - 2 = 6
(9) 10 - 2 = 8
(10) 2 - 1 = 1

① Write the lowercase letters in the table below.

a	b	c	d	e	f
g	h	i	j	k	l
m	n	o	p	q	r
s	t	u	v	w	x
y	z				

DAY 45, pages 89 & 90

❶ What time is it? Write the time under each clock.

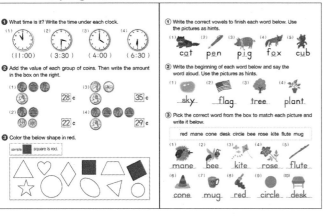

(1) (11:00)
(2) (3:30)
(3) (4:00)
(4) (6:30)

❷ Add the value of each group of coins. Then write the amount in the box on the right.

(1) 28¢
(2) 22¢
(3) 35¢
(4) 29¢

❸ Color the below shape in red.

example: square is red.

① Write the correct vowels to finish each word below. Use the pictures as hints.

(1) cat
(2) pen
(3) pig
(4) fox
(5) cub

② Write the beginning of each word below and say the word aloud. Use the pictures as hints.

(1) sky
(2) flag
(3) tree
(4) plant

③ Pick the correct word from the box to match each picture and write it below.

red mane cone desk circle bee rose kite flute mug

(1) mane
(2) bee
(3) kite
(4) rose
(5) flute
(6) cone
(7) mug
(8) red
(9) circle
(10) desk